THE POWER

OF

Eve

The Revelation in the Garden

Deanna J. Manley

xulon PRESS

Copyright © 2006 by Deanna Manley

The Power of Eve
by Deanna Manley

Printed in the United States of America

ISBN 1-60034-635-9

All rights reserved solely by the author. The author guarantees all contents are original and do not infringe upon the legal rights of any other person or work. No part of this book may be reproduced in any form without the permission of the author. The views expressed in this book are not necessarily those of the publisher.

Unless otherwise indicated, Bible quotations are taken from The Hebrew-Greek Key Study Bible, King James Version. Copyright © 1984, 1991 by AMG International, Inc. Revised edition 1991; The Life Recovery Bible, New Living Translation. Copyright © 1998 by Tyndale House Publishers, Inc.

www.xulonpress.com

Donna,
Thank you for your support and remember to use your influence!
Blessings,
Deanna
2017

DEDICATION

This book is dedicated to the influential men in my life:

To my grandfather, who transitioned into eternal life in 2003, but not without transferring the mantle.

To my father who has loved me unconditionally; thank you for letting me share this revelation with your congregation first.

To my husband, my Adam, for without whom this book would not be possible.

INTRODUCTION

While studying the story of Adam and Eve one Saturday morning, I innocently asked God a question, "Why Eve?" Much to my amazement the answer was not at all what I expected. As I began thinking more in depth about the explanation God had given me, I realized I had just become privy to a revelation I could not keep to myself.

A special power or force readily available to women is revealed through the story of Adam and Eve. When effectively used, this power, or better stated our secret weapon, can literally transform our lives as well as those around us once properly understood and applied.

We actually affect and are affected by people everyday, and whether consciously or unconsciously aware of this supreme energetic force it's at work continually. Oftentimes we use this ability unknowingly while the secular world has tapped into its effectiveness quite successfully.

Not only can this power be used to achieve positive results in our personal lives, the Christian church at large must also seek to understand and utilize this ability in a more effective way. At the eve of this Kingdom Age, the power Eve possessed is necessary artillery for the purpose of establishing the Kingdom of God in the earth. Additionally, this revelation will enable us to reclaim what was forfeited in the garden and restore the dominion we inherited before the "Fall of Man".

My prayer is for you the reader to gain insight and clarity regarding one of the most awesome abilities women possess.

My desire is to see women of all ages and origins set free from the bondages, which have, in some cases, been so deeply rooted in erroneous verbal and subliminal messages from the demonic principalities of this world.

My belief is that once women understand the power given to Eve, they will be equipped to take authority over their lives for the better as daughters of the first woman, first wife and first mother of all humanity.

My challenge is to the Christian church to become empowered as effective witnesses for Christ.

CONTENTS

1. Conditions — Paradise Lost 11
2. Beginnings — Understanding Eve 21
3. The Assignment — Bring Him Back To Me 29
4. High Stakes — The Beguilement of Eve 39
5. Programming — Conformed To This World 47
6. Men — Why Won't He Change? 59
7. Awareness — Expecting What You Accept 73
8. Witchcraft — What the Power of Eve Is Not..............83
9. The Revelation — What Eve Was Given.....................99
10. Factors — How It Works 111
11. Contrasts — Women in the Bible............................127
12. The War — Women and the Church 145

Chapter 1

Conditions — Paradise Lost

The biblical account of Adam and Eve has for some time intrigued me. Their story is mysteriously strange in many ways. Everything was so fresh, so new, unpolluted, uncontaminated and clean...very clean. The trees and foliage must have been plush and green from continual days of warm sunshine. One could only imagine magnificently beautiful flowers painted across hillsides in a colorful assortment of the rainbow. Various species of birds and butterflies flew against powdery blue skies softly decorated with white cottony clouds. An abundance of fruit trees bore luscious ripe fruit. Available vegetation was sufficient to sustain them. Animals of different varieties roamed freely and harmoniously with Adam and Eve. So what really happened that fateful day in Paradise? Why did it happen? I believe the "fall of man" was no fall at all, but a definitive series of events set in motion to eventually bring God glory and give Eve's life real meaning.

Perhaps you've never really thought about this particular aspect of the creation story, but for me the beginning of humanity seems quite extraordinary. The starting point of all human existence begins in a garden, with one man, one woman and then there was this serpent. It's as if God set the stage and characters in a perfectly orchestrated play with a plot that pits evil against good. Of course good appropriately prevails in the end, as any good story line goes, but why did God allow these particular events to transpire? After all, we are talking about real people, real events and one mistake which altered not only the lives of Adam and Eve, but all of humanity for the rest of its existence.

Why Eve? Puzzled by the events in the garden, the answer eluded me for some time. Still other questions ran through my mind as I continued my search for why this scenario played out the way it did. Why was Eve Satan's first human target? In the biblical beginning of God's miraculous creation, Eve was beguiled by the Evil One, not Adam. Furthermore, why were the first mistake and the first sin committed by Eve? Some have concluded she was the weaker vessel, which at first glance appears to be the obvious answer. Or perhaps Adam wasn't paying close enough attention to his wife in order to protect her. What lessons, if any, can we learn from the infamous story in the Garden of Eden? What real purpose did God create women? Lastly, what role, if any, do women have in ending society's continual downward spiral of decay, death, and destruction?

Genesis 3:7(a) — And the eyes of them both were opened. KJV

Because Eve ate of the tree of the knowledge of good and of evil we now understand the difference between good and evil, right and wrong. I would venture to say *we* should also now know better. Eve was our first example of the havoc surely to follow when women disobey God. Of course men share the weight of the blame and they have their judgment from God, but I want to focus on Eve's mistakes, misunderstandings, decisions and ultimate purpose as it relates to women—all women. If we go back to the beginning with

Eve and attempt to understand her actions, her faults and her hidden role in this story, perhaps we can unlock some of the answers to why women do what women do.

Several lessons to be learned from Eve are uncovered in this popular biblical account. Inarguably, she made a seemingly irreversible mistake by committing the first sin. However, something else quite astounding took place in the Garden of Eden besides Eve enduring the pains of childbirth and having to submit to her husband. No, the outcome was not all bad. In fact, something very interesting and cleverly subtle was imparted to women through Eve. Although sin entered into the world, God did not leave us without an essential ability to ensure our victory. To the man God gave commandments, dominion and authority, but to the woman…well just keep reading.

Lamentations 3:51 — Mine eye affecteth mine heart because of all the daughters of my city. KJV

My heart literally aches with unbearable pain seeing countless women in America and the world abroad subjected to and submitted to living considerably less than or contrary to their real potential. Women are many times in relationships and situations not at all conducive to their wellbeing. Our sometimes desperate search for that person or that thing which makes life meaningful has all too often seemed to elude us, while leading us into relationships and circumstances eventually proving painful and destructive. And if the unforeseen vicissitudes of life and the heartache from failed relationships didn't destroy us, we were left at the very least feeling half dead like wounded animals.

We've accepted our lots in life as though we were subject to chance or fate instead of being co-creators with God in making our lives what they were originally ordained and intended to be. Many women are unhappily married while other women are unhappily single, continuing to look for Mr. Right. Several hundreds of thousands of women accept jobs that are demeaning and degrading for the sake of survival. On average women live below the poverty level. In America, the crime rate and subsequent imprisonment of women continues to escalate at a faster pace than for men. Our marriages are failing and our children appear to be out of control, while our government attempts to redefine marriage and regulate the disciplining of our children. Spanking is considered abusive, but we may however legally murder our children by means of abortion. And because good men are supposedly hard to find, you're now permitted to marry another woman if you desire to do so. Women, we are in trouble. We must come to the understanding and awareness of what our role as women of virtue, wives of favor and mothers of God's heritage really means.

Certainly I am saddened and my spirit is deeply troubled because of the many travesties evident in our country today. Not only am I deeply grieved and perplexed, but the following statistics give credence to my despair. Consider these alarming statistics in our current so-called civilized society relative to women. This information has been gathered from various sources in an attempt to bring to light the seriousness of women's issues. Quite frankly our country, communities and families are in desperate need of answers.

The State of the Union

Domestic Violence

Women are being subjected to domestic violence in record numbers. The American Medical Association estimates between 2 to 4 million women are victims of severe assaults by boyfriends or husbands each year. They also estimate 1 of 4 women is likely to be abused by a partner in her lifetime. Furthermore, females are victims of family violence at a rate of at least three times that of males. Studies reveal family violence occurs in at least two million families in the U.S. alone. According to the National Organization for Women, four women are murdered every day in the United States either by their husbands or boyfriends.

Additionally, Caucasian women in America make up 64% of all domestic violence cases. These figures though, are somewhat conservative because battering and assaults are usually not reported until the violence reaches life-threatening proportions. Domestic violence cuts across lines of race, nationality, culture, economics and religion to affect people from all walks of life.

Sexual Exploitation of Women

The sexual exploitation of women in videos, movies, commercials, television shows and various forms of pornography is repulsively shocking. Women are not only being exploited, but are allowing the exploitation. You can only *be* exploited if you permit it in the first place. The pornographic industry is estimated to bring in billions of dollars annually at the expense of women's dignity. Annual rentals and sales of adult videos and DVDs will bring in an estimated $11 billion this year. Additionally, the pornographic industry produces upwards of 11,000 movies each year. Today with more than 2,400 strip clubs in the U.S., some report earnings as high as 8 million dollars annually. Others are employing as many as 200 dancers in their establishments. And if you don't want to visit one of these clubs, you need only to look in your own living room where one third of the family hour television shows contain sexual references and content. Three of the four prime-time networks included sexual innuendo in 2005-2006 season on their programs.

What's more disturbing is the number of Christian men viewing pornography. A recent study determined nearly 33% of male believers are in bondage to some form of pornography. An online survey disclosed 47% of 10,000 Christian men stated pornography was a problem for them in their home. In a "Christianity Today" poll, 44% of pastors admitted to having at least visited an Internet porn site at least once. Currently over 4 million pornographic websites are readily available on the world-wide-web.

Women in Prison

The increase in criminal activity by women and the incarceration of women has risen dramatically in the past 20 years. Statistics taken from U.S. Justice Department's Bureau of Justice Statistics in 1985 approximated 20,000 women in our state and federal prisons. Nearly 18,000 women were in our local jails. By the year 2000 that number had almost quadrupled to 79,000 women incarcerated in state and federal penitentiaries. The number of women in local jails has more than tripled to 60,000. Statistics just recently published by the same reporting agency, determined the total has now exceeded 104,000 women in our state and federal prisons. Moreover 75% of these women are of African-American descent. Additionally, the female prison population has grown by 46% over the past 10 years. In other words, one out of every 1,613 women is incarcerated in the United States.

Amnesty International's report states, "Women tend to commit survival crimes to earn money, feed a drug-dependent lifestyle, and/or escape brutalizing physical conditions and relationships." The chilling reality is when a man goes to prison he loses his freedom, but when a woman goes to prison she loses her freedom and her children. If a woman is pregnant during her incarceration, 24 to 48 hours after delivery she is separated, oftentimes permanently, from her newborn. Another distressful statistic to be noted resulting from this epidemic are the approximately 200,000 children abandoned and adversely affected by their mother's incarceration.

Single-Parent Homes

Single-parent homes are increasing exponentially leaving children to practically raise themselves, while mothers struggle to make ends meet. An estimated 25 million children in the United States are growing up without fathers in the home. In 1998 the average income for single mother households was $18,000 resulting in 6 of every 10 children living near the poverty line. Boys growing up in fatherless homes are two to three times more likely to be involved in crime, drop out of school, and get divorced according to the latest reporting agencies. Girls living without their fathers in the home are two to three times more likely to become pregnant during their teen years and have marriages that end in divorce.

One important footnote, statistically only 5 percent of the single parent population attends church on a regular basis.

Teen Births & Abortions

The number of children born out of wedlock to young teen-mothers is steadily increasing with 445,944 babies born to 15-19 year old girls in 2001. Of this number, nearly one half million children will grow up either on welfare or close to the poverty line because the mother will not have finished high school. Additionally, two-thirds of infants born to teen mothers were fathered by adult men over the age of 20.

More than 1,550,000 abortions were performed last year and is one of the most horrific statistics to date. In other words, almost one of every three pregnancies in America was considered unwanted and subsequently terminated by means of premeditated murder. Stats gathered from the Guttmacher Institute reports this figure has remained constant since the 1980's. This being the case, over 43 million unborn babies have been killed in the past 25 years.

Weight Obsession

Our weight and diet obsessions are also out of control in this country. Diet fads and dieting clinics are for the most part targeting women in their advertising and marketing pitches. The weight-loss industry has been estimated to have had sales of over 43 billion dollars in 2004. This figure includes diet food, diet pills, programs, clinics and camps. What I found interesting in my research of this particular issue is that women living below or just above the poverty level were more likely to be overweight than women with higher incomes. What this means is these same dieting women are less educated. It is not because they are less educated that they tend to be overweight, but their incomes do not afford them to buy foods that are healthier. Organic foods such as fresh vegetables and fruits, as well as choice meats cost more.

Statistically speaking roughly 6 in 10 adults without a high school diploma are overweight according to the Center for Disease Control's National Center for Health Statistics. Additional research from the CDC reported that 63% of men are considered overweight compared to 47% of women. The obesity rate however is about equal with approximately 40 million people falling into this category in the United States.

Eating disorders are at the other end of the spectrum of our weight obsessions. An estimated 6 million women and girls in this country alone, currently struggle with eating disorders and borderline conditions. These include the two most popular, anorexia nervosa and bulimia nervosa.

Okay, now that's the bad news and regrettably not all of it. There are other serious issues relating to women not listed such as sexual assault, HIV/Aids, STD's, drug addiction and alcoholism. These problems are also just as devastating to our society and continue to increase statistically with respect to women.

The above stated issues clearly show the severity of the problems in our society today as they relate to women. Unfortunately, our current societal perplexities have continued to grow and multiply themselves like plagues. The good news is they are however avoidable, preventable and can assuredly be reversed.

The common thread is the specific power at work we must become more aware of. This power or spirit was originally created by God to bring forth positive results beginning with Eve. Satan has however, distorted and perverted its use to the extent we are now living almost barbarically. Just as Eve was seemingly unaware of the trick of Satan, women today as well are unknowingly being beguiled by the lies of the enemy.

I focus on Eve and women collectively, to reveal a truth and make known the reality that the answer to each of these maladies lies within each person of the female persuasion. One thing we can be sure of, these systemic atrocities carry not only the outward manifestation of our internal struggles, but also have a spiritual point of origination as their root cause.

So what do we need to know about this power? First and foremost it's yours, and all persons of the feminine gender posses this particular form of God-ordained power. We have the capability to literally change our current culture as we know it today for the better. Simply by understanding and applying the ability prevalent in women throughout the Bible and recorded in our history books beginning with Eve, we can at the very least change our individual worlds.

In order to make a difference during our lives in this world, in our country, our neighborhoods, our churches and most importantly our homes, we must become empowered with the ability to positively affect others. Realizing you have this power and ability is the first step. Understanding its operation is the second step. And finally, activating the power by means of careful application is the last step.

Chapter 2

Beginnings — Understanding Eve

So what do the issues and statistics in the first chapter have to do with Eve? These statistics substantiate the fact something is going terribly wrong in our society and Eve's decision in the Garden of Eden is where our problems originated. Through careful examination of these staggering numbers and the results stemming from the statistics, we must realize the seriousness and challenges of these problems in need of being addressed respective to women. These issues can only be corrected once we acknowledge them and then take ownership of the fact that we play an integral part in correcting them.

Perhaps the results of our current conditions are perpetuated by not accurately understanding the power Eve possessed. This being the case, many of the atrocities directed towards women in our society remain unchallenged, unchanged and out of control. We will not totally be able to eradicate all of these problems of course, but we can collectively change the course of the continued downward spiral of morals and societal degradation we're facing today.

Understanding Eve's beginning is imperative to help us in better understanding ourselves. Eve was a real human woman like you and I. It's difficult sometimes though, to comprehend the stories and characters in the Bible were actual people and not just fictional accounts of individuals who never existed.

I've attempted to imagine Eve waking up out of a deep sleep suddenly a human being—a woman. It must have been undoubtedly an indescribable, unfathomable experience for her. By starting from the beginning where Eve comes into the picture perhaps we can grasp how we arrived where we are today with respect to the many challenges women are now facing.

To begin with, things don't just happen—that goes without saying. Situations and circumstances in life are set into motion by a series of events. This series of events is called "the process". Secondly we can't hope to change the outcome or results in our lives without first understanding what is going on prior to the process, within the process and the end result of the process. Furthermore, these particular issues were selected bringing to the forefront what many women have gone through or are currently experiencing as a result of the process of life and the choices we've made.

After some unreported number of blissful days, months or even years in the Garden of Eden, Satan just showed up. Eve didn't know him and was unaware of his motives. She appears to have acted in an almost naïve childlike way as she made conversation with him. Eve's story provides insight to the vulnerabilities and frailties of our human nature and the dangers of giving place to the devil.

Before she ate of "the tree" sin had not yet entered the world. Eve however, seemed to have been struggling in her mind with her flesh as Satan presented his cunning argument to her. After her conversation with the serpent, Eve's actions give the appearance of being premeditated. From her actions, it would be fair to deduce the possibility of sin was already in the world prior to her arrival or Satan's emergence in the garden. Eve's carnal nature, which was part of her original composition, caused her to sin. Her initial thoughts during her encounter with the serpent were the first part of "the process". Satan initially attacks her beliefs. In fact, his opening statement to Eve wasn't a statement at all, but a seductive question.

Genesis 3:1 — Now the serpent was more subtle than any beast of the field which the Lord God had made. And he said unto the woman, "Yea, hath God said, 'Ye shall not eat of every tree of the garden?'" KJV

Satan activated, posing this question to Eve, her thinking and reasoning faculties. If Satan could cause her to question or reconsider her beliefs, he could possibly cause her to change her mind about what she believed.

The next step in the process of Eve's beguilement was her decision to have conversation with Satan. Though she put up a good argument, Eve was persuaded to the point of believing what he was saying. We too, receive negative information each and every day from outside sources as well as from the internal conversations we have with ourselves. How we process the negative information determines our results. Our decisions or choices based on the information received becomes the important catalyst to the outcome of life-changing matters and is the second part of "the process". The question Eve had to answer was quite simple as it is for us—do we believe God or not? Satan ensnared Eve during the decision-making process once the thought process was initiated convincing her to disbelieve what God had commanded.

Our basic belief systems are established during our childhood years. Development, adjustments and alterations of our belief systems continue throughout our lives. Eve however was at a disadvantage. She was not birthed through the womb of a mother and entered the world already an adult. She missed the critical formative years—the nurturing of her mother and father—no siblings to contend with—no grandparents to spoil her—and no other man to choose but Adam. She would not experience the first day of school, have a favorite teacher or attend her high school prom. Eve didn't experience playing with dolls or other children and didn't learn to share as a toddler. With only one rule to obey, she didn't even get that right! There weren't any governmental laws established or 10 commandments from Moses for her to adhere to—just one rule. And if Eve couldn't obey the only law given to her by God, where does this leave us?

Eve's downfall actually came before she ate of the fruit. She first thought about what Satan was saying and was then convinced to the point of agreement. This is important to note because we would not commit sin if our minds were not in agreement with the sin. We are triune beings, that is to say, spirit, soul and body. When the mind and body are in agreement concerning a decision, the spirit becomes outnumbered and overruled. Thus, we will ultimately commit sin. This is what happened to Eve. She came into agreement with Satan through her reasoning, yielded to her flesh and consequently made the decision to sin. On the other hand, the possibility and our ultimate goal should be for our spirits and our minds to be in agreement. Our flesh or our carnal nature is overruled when our spirits and minds are in agreement and sin becomes disannulled.

Romans 7:25 — So then with the mind I serve the law of God; but with the flesh the law of sin. KJV

I Corinthians 9:27 — I discipline my body and bring it into subjection. KJV

The Apostle Paul is referring to bringing ones body into alignment with the spirit and mind. Agreement of mind with the body is the third stage in "the process". Your body can only do what your mind instructs it to do. When your spirit is controlling your thoughts, your actions will result in temperance and restraint. The devil knew this vital part of "the process". Unfortunately, Eve did not.

Once the decision to sin has been made through the mind and the body is in agreement, the next stage is the action stage. Eve takes the forbidden fruit and eats it. She had been seduced into thinking about eating the fruit and the benefits it could provide. Her mind then instructed her hand to pick the fruit off of the "tree" and take a bite. Her body and mind are now in agreement. The book of James explains it this way:

James 1:14-15 — But each one is tempted when he is drawn away by his own desires and enticed. Then when desire has conceived, it gives birth to sin; and sin when it is full-grown, brings forth death. KJV

From James' teaching we can conclude the existence of an innate ability in each of us to know the difference between what is good and evil, right or wrong because of the "tree". Making the right choices can be accomplished by analyzing the consequences or the outcome of our decisions before the actual decision is made. This is the last phase of "the process" which yields our results and produces our circumstances. All too often we do one of two things when making a decision. We either act first, usually based on some fleshly need or desire and deal with the consequences later, no matter how devastating they may be; or, we create some unrealistic fantasy in our minds of the desired outcome which leads to disappointment when our imagined results are not realized.

On a daily basis we process thousands and thousands of thoughts consciously and subconsciously and depending upon our choices, we ultimately create our results. It's vitally important to think about what you are thinking about. Your thoughts throughout each day will determine how each of your days is spent. We see through Eve, just how important it is to think important decisions through as carefully as possible.

Further examination of the sequence of events in the Garden of Eden will help us to understand what happens after just one bad decision is made. Following the initial sin, eating of the forbidden fruit, another decision then becomes necessary. Eve and her husband together make the decision to run and hide. Although God had not yet confronted Adam and Eve, they knew they were wrong. Assuredly other sins will usually follow in an attempt to cover up the original sin. Eve had opened the door to the demonic world and sin steps in to take dominion over mankind. And though the possibility of sin may have been present in the world prior to the creation of man, it could have only been manifested through man. The significance of this reality is that mankind can only commit sin. The devil is incapable of making us do anything.

Most of the time we know what is wrong before we choose to do wrong, yet commit sin anyway. It's usually because we do not seriously consider or understand the consequences of our actions. Had Eve known her decision to do wrong would hurt God, her husband, herself, her unborn children and generations to come, she probably would have at least thought twice about taking what was deemed impermissible.

The inevitability of consequence is another lesson we can draw from these events. Eve did not thoroughly think through the possible outcome of her decisions nor did she know the curses to follow would take place. She proceeded to sin without much caution or consideration. God did not explain to Adam or Eve in entirety the judgment to befall them until afterwards. Usually we don't know the extent a bad decision can have on our lives until it's too late. Without Eve knowing the end results of her decision we can see how easy it was for Eve to make such a hasty choice. What God did tell them is they would die, which they eventually did. But what God didn't tell them beforehand was they would suffer during their lives before they died. That almost doesn't seem fair, but God will oftentimes only give us what we need to know and leave the decision to obey Him up to us.

Genesis 3:13 — And the Lord God said unto the woman, "What is this that thou hast done?" And the woman said, "The serpent beguiled me, and I did eat." KJV

Once God confronted Adam and Eve, in an attempt to cover up their sin, they cast the blame on someone else. Adam blamed Eve and Eve blames the serpent. She then however acknowledges it was the decision *she* made and subsequent action *she* took as the real cause of her dilemma with God. Herein lies the first step to the answer of our problems and situations—acknowledgement. Acknowledgement is the required key and the first step to correcting wrong decisions. Eve uses the beguilement of the serpent as her excuse, but then plainly admits, "I did eat".

The second step, once we acknowledge where we are wrong, is to determine change is necessary. Eve didn't get a second chance to correct her mistake. She didn't have the option of salvation through Jesus Christ, which provides forgiveness of sin or repentance. We, however, have the benefit of grace and opportunity to ask for forgiveness from God through salvation. Because we have the privilege of choice, we also have the ability to alter our direction, change our thinking and correct wrong decisions.

Eve's story helped me discover the root cause of my former problems with men, drugs and alcohol. I too, had received incorrect information. Without fully understanding the consequences, I was making major life-changing and destructive choices based on what I thought to be true. I also blamed others for the choices I made. Though Eve and I had a different set of circumstances we both have at least 4 things in common—we were both disobedient to God; we both rejected what we already knew to be the truth; Eve and I also suffered in the throws of denial; and most importantly, we contributed to our husbands' downfall. Eve was not totally to blame for Adam's sin, nor was I for my husband's mistakes, but she and I were both unquestionably an accessory.

Chapter 3

The Assignment — Bring Him Back To Me

Twenty years ago after meeting my husband, I remember having a conversation with him about God, religion and the church early on in our relationship. I can recall it vividly as if it were yesterday. During our conversation God was also participating. When He speaks you don't forget it. Interrupting our conversation, God whispered these profound words to me, *"This is your assignment; bring him back to me."*

Mind you at the time, I was not attending church, although I had been raised in a Christian home. My relationship with God had become almost non-existent during my early twenties. Even though I wasn't in fellowship with God, I always knew He was there. Several years would pass before these prophetic words of instruction would come to fruition in my life. I never, however, forgot those words. As the years passed, I would from time to time recall the instruction I had received from God, *"This is your assignment; bring him back to me."* Because of these words of instruction, I was unable to leave my husband prior to our deliverance, although many times I wanted to.

Throughout the first ten years of our relationship, my husband and I were heavily involved in drugs and alcohol. I just couldn't see how God expected *me* to turn things around, especially since things looked so bleak. The first three years were spent in the chaotic and destructive world of cocaine abuse, which by the way was something I never thought I would do. After becoming addicted, cocaine's grip continued to have such an incredible hold on me. I was afraid I would never escape, let alone be able to rescue someone else. Many times in the early stages of our relationship, I wondered if I was really in love with my husband or in love with the drugs he supplied me. He knew where all the drug spots were and made the purchases. Most of the time, I would go with him to get the drugs, but never had the courage to actually buy them myself.

I dreaded the thought of dying in my addictive lifestyle. Sometimes it felt as though my heart was going to explode during episodes of getting high. I hated what I was doing. Depression had taken over my mind and I wasn't making good choices. Cocaine's power over me was relentless. Breaking free appeared impossible. While watching a televangelist one day desperately trying to receive my deliverance, I remember laying my hands on the television and praying, hoping God would hear me, but to no avail. From time to time, I would try to read my Bible, but that didn't work either. I couldn't seem to understand all that King James English. Even when I prayed, I didn't think God was listening or even knew I existed.

After about three years of using cocaine, my husband and I started experimenting with heroin. At first I didn't realize what I was getting myself into. Just like Eve I was so naïve to the trap Satan had set for me. In retrospect, I only managed to trade one drug for another, and for the next seven years had an ongoing affair with heroin. It became my best friend as well as my dictator and slave master. Heroin told me when to get up, where to go and what to do. Amazingly, we were both able to maintain our professional jobs for some time. We had become what I refer to as "professional junkies", working to get high and getting high so we could work.

Over the course of time, we sunk so low practically losing everything. Not only were we addicted to drugs; we became addicted to each other. We were drug partners. In some strange, twisted way we grew comfortable with what we were doing because we were doing it 'together'. The drugs taught us how to manipulate and control each other too. When my husband had money, he controlled me. If I had money then I controlled him and the drugs controlled and manipulated both of us.

In May of 1992, we decided to get married. We lived together, a.k.a. "shacking up", for the first seven years of our relationship. What prompted us to marry was our attempt to get our lives in order. Thank God for having grown up in Christian homes where godly values were instilled in us. Although we had veered far away from our upbringing, we could no longer continue living together unmarried. We both knew better and knew it wasn't right. We were also well aware of the fact that our drug addiction wasn't right either. What we didn't know was Satan was not at all in favor of us getting married or getting off of drugs.

We married on May 23, 1992. Within two weeks after our wedding, a fire broke out in our home destroying what little we had and resulted in our becoming homeless. The Red Cross assisted us for the first few weeks providing temporary housing. Afterwards, we moved into a tiny motel room because we couldn't qualify or afford to get into an apartment. Our credit had been damaged due to our drug use and we didn't have any immediate savings.

Two days after moving into this somewhat rundown motel, we were awakened in the middle of the night by the fire department. Not only were our living quarters cramped, but this roadside lodge was also in a flood zone. On this particular night, a massive rain cloud fixed itself directly over the motel. In a short period of time, it rained so hard and so fast flooding the entire grounds. A fireman, frantically knocking on our door, insisted we evacuate. When we opened the door, water in the parking lot was knee deep. We threw our belongings in the bathtub, gathered our children and waded to our car. As we opened the car door, water poured in flooding out our only means of transportation. In a matter of weeks we had been through a fire and now a flood. (I have a special appreciation for the song that declares, "I've come through the fire and been through the flood").

We moved to another motel offering rooms to rent, this one shabbier than the first. The next month and a half we lived there with our two children. What a way to start a marriage! Eventually, it dawned on us we had access to money saved through our retirement plans on our jobs. We found a home with an assumable loan and made the purchase. Fortunately at that time, assumable loans didn't require credit approval, only a small down payment.

This was now August of 1992 and during the closing of our home, as I was signing the papers, this sick feeling, a premonition of sorts overwhelmed me. Because of our drug addiction, I knew this was not a home I would live in for very long. Nevertheless, I signed the papers.

Additional monies were left over from our closing and my husband's addiction grew worse. I watched him spend over $7000 in a matter of weeks. Once the money ran out his dependency for the drugs could only be arrested through hospitalization. He could no longer work without being high. Withdrawal symptoms were making him quite ill. In order to get the proper help, he had to confess to his employer the nature of his condition.

In September 1992, his job sent him to a drug and alcohol rehabilitation facility in Texas. There he spent twenty-one days in a substance abuse program, first in detox and then in recovery. I still had to hold down the fort at home and actually attempted to stop using drugs while he was gone. Unfortunately, I was in denial that I needed professional help as well. When my husband returned home, the addiction for both of us did too. Now he was under a microscope at work and things progressed from bad to worse...much worse. About six months later, my husband lost his job. It was now February 1993.

One Thursday evening in March of that same year, we were about to experience something we would both live to regret and remember for the rest of our lives. I worked the evening shift and once again, my husband had been late picking me up from work. When he finally showed up, two other men were with him. One was white and the other was black. The black man was a drug associate of ours named Dwight, but this white man was a stranger, someone my husband picked up somewhere on the street.

We drove to a drug-house we frequented and proceeded to get high. While in the same room with this young man, he began talking about his life. He had just been released from a drug rehabilitation center and mentioned he had a fiancé. As he was mixing up a large amount of cocaine in a spoon with some water, he continued discussing his future plans, which included marriage. He proudly showed me a black and white picture of his soon-to-be bride. She was very pretty.

I noticed as I studied this young man's face, his beautiful blue piercing eyes stood out complimenting his dark hair. He was about 6'4", in his latter twenties and quite attractive. Perhaps a football player during his high school days, his physique suggested he was athletic. I also remember how shocked I was watching him run that entire syringe of cocaine up his arm. I had never before seen anyone shoot up such a large amount of cocaine at one time.

The Power of Eve

After a few hours passed we decided to leave. This white stranger rode home with us along with our friend Dwight. The original plan was to give this guy a ride home, but we didn't have enough charge in our car's battery to make it to his house. Because the alternator was not functioning, the car was operating off of the battery. We decided to let everyone sleep at our home until the morning. I later discovered that my husband thought our new acquaintance had more drugs and planned to buy some from him in the morning.

Once we arrived at our house, we gave our guests a brief tour of our home. I made palettes on the floor of our living room for Dwight and this stranger. Before going upstairs to bed, our visitor asked me where the bathroom was. I politely pointed to the one downstairs. As he was closing the door to the bathroom, I said goodnight. Attempting to go to sleep, my husband and I heard this young man snoring very loudly. The walls seemed to be shaking with his thunderously loud, heavy breathing. We managed somehow to drown him out enough to fall asleep. Downstairs in the living room with our noisy guest, Dwight fought with trying to get some sleep as well.

The next morning my husband was rushing around getting our oldest daughter off to school. After she left for school, he came upstairs and awakened me to the worst news I could have ever imagined. My husband's face was very serious and somewhat pale as he softly said, "Dee, you're not going to believe this…that guy is dead". I quickly sat up in my bed and pleaded with my husband, "Come on Bunk please don't tell me that!" Repeating himself to me again, "He's dead, Dee." I put my glasses on, jumped out of bed and grabbed my robe to see for myself. As I turned the corner of the kitchen, my eyes were drawn to the image in the floor. In total disbelief I stared at the body, hoping he would move or at least breathe. After a few moments of trying to collect my thoughts, I forced my mind come to grips with this tragic reality. A complete stranger was lying in my living floor dead. A small pool of blood on the carpet had come from his mouth as he bled to death internally from a drug overdose. His skin color had turned blue, his hair was disheveled and rigormortis had set in.

I looked at my husband and asked in a panic, "What are we going to do?" Here we were three black drug addicts, living in a predominately white neighborhood, with a dead white man in our house. How would we explain what had happened and not be charged with murder? While my husband and Dwight were contemplating how to dispose of the body, my thoughts were consumed with getting that dead man out of my house. I went back upstairs, hurriedly put on my clothes and went to the nearest payphone to call the police. On the way to the convenience store, I made conversation with myself, "Surely we could simply explain to the police 'he just died'. They would remove the corpse and that would be the end of it." How could I have known that once the police arrived they would immediately suspect us of foul play? Who could blame them?

Shortly after calling 911, four squad cars pulled up in front of my home. The officers quickly separated us and questioned us briefly. Evidently, whatever each of us was saying wasn't adding up and they soon took us downtown for further interrogation. In the meantime, additional detectives arrived to continue thoroughly searching our home for additional clues as to what had actually transpired.

I attempted to lie to the investigators at first, but as the questions continued and the minutes became hours, I started to break. The detectives weren't buying our stories. Why would we pick up this complete stranger and allow him to sleep over night in our house? They also found evidence of our drug use during their search of our home. After several hours passed, I finally explained to the police how we met this person and the events that led up to his death. Fortunately,

I recalled the conversation with this young man the night before. He told me that if he ever decided to commit suicide, it would be by overdosing on drugs. I told the police about this conversation, having no idea this young stranger made the same statement to Dwight earlier that evening. Dwight informed the police 'our guest' went into the downstairs bathroom and must have injected the rest of his drugs. To this day we don't know how much he used, but we do know it was enough to kill him. Mind you, I had already seen the deceased use a large amount of cocaine only hours earlier.

Our stories finally corroborated with each other. Because of the statements made to us prior to the death of this young man concerning suicide, the police ruled it as such and released us. You would have thought we would have been scared enough to stop using drugs after this episode, but it only gave us another excuse to continue our escape from reality.

Several years have passed since this horrible experience. Two things still haunt me though about the apparent suicide of this young man. I'll never forget the sound of the death rattle we mistook for just loud snoring; the other is—I can't remember his name.

One month after this terrible incident, I lost my job. We took the rest of our savings from our 401K's and lived off of the money until the money ran out. In total, my husband and I spent about $30,000 in a very short period of time. We did manage, however, to pay our mortgage in advance for the next several months to avoid foreclosure and eviction. Though we had housing, we were oftentimes living with no electricity and/or water.

By the summer of 1994, foreclosure proceedings had been initiated and we were being evicted from our home. The premonition I had upon our purchasing this home was now coming to pass. Prior to our eviction, my husband had landed himself in jail for failing to appear in court on previous misdemeanor charges. Very much alone, I had no car, no phone and no lights. What little water we had access to we were stealing from our neighbors. To make matters all the more complicated, I was six months pregnant with my third child.

One evening prior to becoming homeless, I prayed to God one more time. It wasn't a long prayer—it didn't have to be. I've learned over the years prayers don't have to be lengthy, only effective. "God if you're there", I prayed, "I need you right now! Please help me! God, if you don't help me, I don't know what I'm going to do", I pleaded. Miraculously, my life began to completely turn around the very next day. It was as if I was stepping out of one world and into another.

We had recently met a Christian couple through one of our associates. I called them to help me put what was left of my belongings into storage. Not only did they come to my aid, they brought others with them. We boxed up my things, loaded them into the truck and put them into storage. They also offered to take my children and me in to their home. I was so very grateful to them because the alternative for me would have been a shelter.

God knew I was broken. He also knew I was tired of the way I was living. We started attending church with the family that had taken us in. It became immediately apparent to me they were truly living what they believed. Their house was so peaceful. Seizing the opportunity afforded me I started reading my Bible with great fervency. I was actually able to understand the King James Version English! My eyes were now being opened and the possibility of living a better life was more real to me than it had been in a long time. I also contacted the local drug rehabilitation center and enrolled in an outpatient recovery program. So many people God sent my way helped me get well. The road to recovery however was not an easy one and my husband didn't stop using drugs just because I did.

Just as Eve's one mistake cost her dearly, my one wrong decision to use drugs just one time cost me as well. There are ten precious years of my life I can never get back or undo, not to mention the neglect suffered by my children. And I won't even try to calculate the lost money. I'm not at all attempting to validate my behavior or Eve's, but the real issue is that something greater was and is at stake for Eve and for me. Satan was after something that day in Paradise. He has been after something in my life too. That "something" didn't just belong to Eve, but I realized I too was carrying a gift, a weapon and an ability, which was passed down through history from God and it all started with Eve. There was and still is much at stake.

Chapter 4

High Stakes — The Beguilement of Eve

Why Satan Beguiled Eve

Why didn't the serpent just kill Eve or Adam? It's not as though he couldn't have killed her. He was a serpent, a snake. He may have possibly had venomous fangs. With one swift bite Eve would have surely died. The Bible is not specific though, if the devil was a poisonous serpent. Or maybe he was of the constrictor type and could have wrapped himself around her smothering her to death. Genesis also doesn't tell us God forbade Satan from killing Eve. So what was Satan's real mission? Why did the devil only settle for seducing her to sin? We know Satan is God's enemy and he hates God. But why didn't Satan just destroy God's creation before Adam and Eve begin to procreate and populate the earth as they had been commanded to do?

The devil wanted Eve dead of course and he wanted me dead too. Satan was angry with God and jealous of the communion mankind had with Him. The serpent didn't kill Eve because he couldn't, but he concluded it would be a

The Power of Eve

much bigger to blow to God if she destroyed herself. His ultimate goal was to get Eve to kill herself! Of course! What an under-minded plan. What a perfect plot! Satan would have been completely vindicated had he been successful in causing God's own creation to destroy itself. What a smack in the face to God this would be, at least that's what Satan had to be thinking. The creation, fearfully and wonderfully made by God Almighty self-destructs! If Eve commits suicide what greater pain could Satan inflict upon the God that had the audacity to cast him out of heaven? Satan didn't have to hand her the fruit or force it in her mouth. The sly serpent only used a cleverly crafted lie and Eve bought and bit into it.

The sad truth is many of us are killing ourselves today as well. Overeating, over-stressing, over-working, oversexed, over-stimulated, and over-indulging in many areas is killing us and we think it's the devil. Yes, he starts the ball rolling by feeding us lies, but like Eve, we're assisting him and we are the ones suffering the consequences, not Satan. We must also understand the devil has a two-fold purpose, first to make God a liar and secondly to keep us from finding out the truth. The enemy's plan to keep us from the truth is only successful when we are ignorant of the truth causing us to fall prey to his lies as Eve did.

How Satan Beguiled Eve

The issue of "how Satan beguiled Eve" is just as important as why Satan beguiled Eve. Through further investigation of Genesis chapter 3 we find Eve's desire, godliness, knowledge and vision were all being tempted that particular day in the garden. Jesus, in an undeniably identical sequence of events was tempted in the wilderness in the same areas. Careful review of Matthew 4 records the devil came to tempt Jesus after forty days of fasting. The very same tactics he used with Eve and Jesus are the same tactics he uses on us in an attempt to destroy our lives. He has no new tricks—he doesn't need any. Eve reveals to us exactly what is at stake. Jesus shows us the way to victory.

The first temptation was food. Satan's lure with Eve was the fruit and with Jesus it was with bread. Food symbolically is directly associated with the appetite, hunger and our passions. What Eve was hungry for or desired was completely tied to her appetite because you become what you eat. In other words, whatever deception you take in, you will manifest that particular behavior. Likewise, whatever truth you digest, you will exhibit that corresponding behavior.

Additionally, I find it interesting fruit was the object of the temptation with Eve. The fruit Eve ate first was actually the fruit of Satan's lips. His lie and deceit was enough to convince Eve to sin. Furthermore, fruit represents four very significant terms in the Bible. Over 200 references to fruit can be found in the scriptures. To begin with, when God created fruit He gave it the ability to reproduce after its own kind.

Genesis 1:11 — And God said, "Let the earth bring forth grass, the herb yielding seed, and the fruit tree yielding fruit after his kind, whose seed is in itself, upon the earth"; and it was so. KJV

This is not only true for natural fruit yielding from trees and such, but relative to mankind it refers to our offspring, our labor, our speech or conversation and our spirit. After Eve ate of the forbidden fruit her seed/children/fruit of her womb, became imperfect, tainted and flawed. When Adam ate of this same prohibited fruit, his responsibility of working became difficult and burdensome. Adam and Eve's spirits were also affected with respect to their relationship with God, no longer walking in peace with their Creator.

The Power of Eve

They hid themselves and were ashamed to stand in the presence of God. The last inference to fruit, the fruit of their lips, changed from them being truthful to now casting the blame on each other and lying to God.

Satan was quite knowledgeable of the importance of the fruit. He understood the law of genetics as well, that a seed will produce after its own kind. If the seed is defective, it will bear defective fruit. This process can and will be perpetuated indefinitely until the seed is altered, transformed, redirected or destroyed.

Had Eve only taken the one word or commandment of God she knew, she would not have fallen prey to Satan's deceptive tactic. She may not have actually been hungry, but the persuasiveness of the enemy's ad campaign made her think that she was. Notice Eve's conclusion to the lie;

Genesis 3:6 — And when the woman <u>saw</u> that the tree was good for food, and that it was pleasant to the eye, and a tree to be desired to make one wise, she took of the fruit thereof, and did eat, and gave also unto her husband with her; and he did eat. KJV

Simply stated, she stopped, listened, looked and then took. The totality of the temptation was all tied to Eve's appetite—not for the fruit, but for what the fruit could provide. The word **saw** in this portion of scripture refers to being able to see intellectually or to reason. We now understand how easy it is to be convinced to make wrong decisions based on our appetites and/or desire once our reasoning, judgment and perception is swayed. The tendency of being somewhat naïve and gullible at times when it comes to our hunger or desire for things we may think we need or want can prove detrimental to our well-being.

The second subtle strategy was to deceive Eve into believing she wasn't already as God. The tactic the enemy

The Power of Eve

used, the "if only" argument, brings to light the question of Eve's godliness or completeness.

Genesis 3:5 — (The serpent speaking to Eve) "For God doth know that in the day ye eat thereof, then your eyes shall be opened and ye shall be as gods, knowing good and evil." KJV

Satan had to devise a fail-proof lie. He not only brings into question Eve's godliness, but also leads her to believe perhaps God is limiting her or keeping something from her. Satan's goal was to convince Eve to become dissatisfied with who she was thereby insulting the sovereignty of God. The devil knew this lie could work and would work. He had already proven it through the other angels that were cast out of heaven with him. And because he no longer has any persuasion with the angels in heaven, he's turned his attentions on God's creation. The next verse of scripture records the very words used by Satan, which caused his banishment from heaven.

Isaiah 14:14 — I will ascend above the heights of the clouds; I will be like the most High. KJV

If Satan knew anything, he knew any attempt by man or angel to become God or above God would result in certain expulsion from God's presence. He used this persuasive tactic with Eve because this same rebellious thinking tripped him up, which led to his permanent removal from heaven. Satan's dissatisfaction with his position in heaven resulted in eternal repercussions for him. Lucifer's desire was to be like God and equal to God. He persuaded Eve that she too should have the same desire. Eve's deception, dissatisfaction with how God had created her and her disobedience, caused her dismissal from the presence of God.

The propensity towards this somewhat erroneous way of thinking is unproductive to say the least and can greatly hinder our relationship with God. Guilt, self-condemnation, dissatisfaction and inner torment robs us of enjoying our lives. If only I were 20 pounds lighter, if only I was younger or older, if only I had more money, if only I had a man, if only... if only... if only...then I would be happy, complete or whole. The devil told Eve if she ate of the tree of knowledge she would be as a god. This caused her to think in the "if only" mindset, not realizing she was already as God. God had made her in his image! The "if only" mindset steals from us the very precious commodity called time. It also causes us to miss out on the blessings of each and every day.

The enemy uses this bit of arsenal to point out what we don't have. This tactic revealed to Eve what she didn't possess and convinced her it was something she needed. The devil also attempted this same strategy with Jesus in the wilderness. Compare the next two verses of scripture in their parallelism:

Genesis 3:6 — And when the woman saw that the tree was good for food, and that <u>it was pleasant to the eye, and a tree to be desired to make one wise</u>, she took of the fruit thereof, and did eat. KJV

Matthew 4:8-9 — Again, the devil taketh him up into an exceeding high mountain, and <u>showed him all the kingdoms of the world, and the glory of</u> them; and saith unto him, "All of these things will I give thee." KJV

Eve's desire to become wise and her believing that she wasn't already wise proves the cleverness of Satan's tongue. Furthermore, Jesus' godliness was questioned and His deity was challenged, not once but twice. Jesus however knew Satan couldn't give him something he already had. And because Jesus very well knew who He was, responds to Satan by telling him not to tempt God.

Matthew 4:5-7 — Then the devil taketh him up into the holy city, and setteth him on a pinnacle of the temple, and saith unto him, <u>If thou be the Son of</u> <u>God</u>, cast thyself down: for it is written, He shall give his angels charge concerning thee: and in their hands they shall bear thee up, lest at any time thou dash thy foot against a stone. Jesus said unto him, "It is written again, Thou shalt not tempt the Lord thy God". KJV

The third area the devil attempts to defeat us is in the area of our knowledge of the Word of God. Satan blatantly tells Eve she will not die if she eats of the fruit. The devil is basically calling God a liar and in a very clever way, tells Eve she doesn't know what she's talking about. Eve goes as far as quoting the commandment back to Satan, which was evidence she *did* know what God had instructed. Unfortunately she allowed that sly serpent to suggest otherwise.

Genesis 3:2-3 — And <u>the woman said</u> unto the serpent, We may eat of the fruit of the trees of the garden: but of the fruit of the tree which is in the midst of the garden, God hath said, Ye shall not eat of it, neither shall ye touch it, lest ye die. KVJ

How many times are we guilty of knowing the Word of God, quoting the Word of God, but still don't believe it? Eve is our first example of the war ensuing with every Christian. She should have and could have rebuked Satan or at least walked away. But she stayed in a negative situation too long and it regrettably got the best of her.

Jesus on the other hand, wasted no more of His time debating with Satan regarding the Word of God because He was the Word. Jesus and Eve both show us the importance of knowing God's Word. Eve could have rebuked Satan, but was unaware of her enemy or her authority. Jesus simply commands the devil to leave. Jesus and Eve also help us to see that winning over the enemy is only possible through accurate knowledge of your Bible. Jesus exhibits his wisdom and knowledge of the scriptures, rebukes the devil and refuses to be so easily tricked. We can further conclude the devil left tempting Jesus because he ran out of tricks!

We now know the "why" and the "how" of Eve's temptation resulting in her ultimate downfall. We can also clearly see the end result of the process of Eve's original sin. The "why" and "how" also provides explanation of her beguilement and subsequent banishment from the garden. In addition to the lies the enemy uses, spiritual forces contribute to the perpetuation of these lies. Their effects are evident throughout our society today. Identifying those forces is the next stage towards better equipping ourselves for the purpose of further empowerment.

Chapter 5

Programming — Conformed To This World

We live in the land of the free and the home of the brave. Our freedom is the most precious commodity we have, but people are in bondage to so many various things. Understanding and awareness of the world system's conditioning and psychological programming is necessary in order to obtain true freedom thereby improving our lives. The word of the Lord assures us,

I Corinthians 2:12 & 14 — Now we have received, not the spirit of the world, but the spirit which is of God; that we might know the things that are freely given to us of God. v.14 – But the natural man receiveth not the things of the Spirit of God: for they are foolishness unto him: neither can he know them, because they are spiritually discerned. KJV

God's Word informs us that these "things" He has given to us are spiritually discerned. When our minds are in agreement with our spirit, we then make the right decisions through the vehicle of discernment. We covered that in the previous chapters. Furthermore, discernment is a deciphering of information leading to knowledge, revelation and making the right choices. Eve did not utilize her discernment with the serpent and we can see the lack of its proper use has at times entrapped many of us. This enslavement has undoubtedly taken place in the mind through the subtle programming techniques of the "world system".

We have countless opportunities at our disposal in this country. We can live wherever we chose, drive the automobile we desire, obtain education and employment according to our aspirations and make more money than we can ever spend. Yet, sometimes we find ourselves living as victims in defeat and failure. Of course with the help of the media feeding us with negativity, greed, fear and lies, it's as if some other force is at work intent upon us staying bound.

The World System

Romans 12:2 — Be not conformed to this world but be ye transformed by the renewing of your mind. KJV

The Apostle Paul strongly admonishes us against becoming conformed to this world and to renew our minds by taking on the mind of Christ. We have however, gradually become desensitized to the travesties around us. It's as if the human race has been lulled to sleep by something we can't quite put our finger on.

The truth of the matter is many of us have become conformed to this "world system" to the point of hopelessness, depression, discouragement and apathy. Conformity seems to be the easier rode to take as opposed to being different. Because women have a natural predisposition of pleasing others and submitting is easier than confrontation, we oftentimes make the wrong decisions for our lives for the sake of conformity. Conforming to the "world system" has gradually led us into mediocrity, complacency and unhappiness. Because of the programming of our current society and the negative forces at work through the "world system", many of the circumstances women are facing seem perpetually insurmountable.

Allowing circumstances we should strongly object happens because society as a whole has continued to move further away from God. Acceptance of particular behaviors and lifestyles once considered taboo, have now become the norm. Some examples of what's become all too acceptable in today's society are premarital sex, abortion, cohabitation, homosexuality and having a child or children out of wedlock. Certainly the media and various forms of entertainment have helped us gradually accept these behaviors as expressions of our freedom. It becomes necessary then for us to identify the subliminal messages and subtleties we have received and accepted from a society governed by demonic principalities.

We are literally being bombarded with hundreds of thousands of commercials, newspaper and magazine advertisements, junk mail and Internet spam. Much of advertising is an attempt to get us to conform to our world. Although money from sales is the goal, the driving force working behind the scenes of all ad campaigns is vying for your money, your mind and your life. This is referred to as the "world system".

The way in which the news is reported is an example in which we've become at least partially numb. In fact, a popular cliché amongst news reporters is "if it doesn't bleed, it doesn't lead". When a murder is aired as the top-leading story, reporters give the depressing details with very little emotion. Plainly giving us the particulars, they casually go on to the next story. The only time you see any display of emotion during the news broadcast is when a victim's family members or their neighbors are interviewed. This strategy is used to cause the ratings to increase, often referred to as sensationalism. We watch intently and shake our heads; not realizing that day after day of watching such horrific and depressing news is actually making us fearful and insensitive to the world around us. This method of reporting the news is not at all unintentional on the part of the media.

The same holds true for other forms of television viewing where sex, crimes of all types, offensive language and other forms of ridiculous behavior have become standard. Then add to the list movies, videos, video games and musical lyrics overrun with violence, vulgarities and nudity and you can hardly escape from being affected and infected negatively by all of these so-called forms of entertainment.

Furthermore, as stated in chapter 1, women are many times being exploited and degraded in most of these "art forms". Two seemingly harmless game shows in particular come to mind as we look at the subliminal messages being transmitted through our televisions. The first show has an infamous consonant and vowel turning woman, while the other game show exploits four women a.k.a. Barker's Beauties. Have you ever wondered why these particular women are needed? Are they really necessary to the success of these shows? They certainly aren't there to entertain women in America. They gracefully parade around on stage rarely ever speaking, in basically mindless jobs, without considering the messages they are really sending. And millions of Americans watch these shows without realizing the messages they are receiving. Additionally, women are all too often used as bait in commercials and television programs to persuade men to tune in. Women are also used to promote and sell a variety of products. Marketing experts recognize women are not only able to seduce men to make purchases, but women are able to persuade each other to spend money as well.

Through systematic programming, the same falsehoods that Eve fell for have caused us to be conformed to this world. The lie being, we are not good enough the way God created us. God did not create Eve to be Adam's showpiece or his property. The "world system" however, has perverted the woman's role. It attempts to dictate to us who we are, what we should have, what we should look like and what we should desire, always taking great care to remind us of what and where we are lacking.

One message in particular being transmitted to women through the media is we're not pretty enough or sexy enough. Comparing ourselves with the "average" female in magazines, commercials, beauty pageants, movies and videos will surely lead to low self-esteem and possibly depression. Then we sit on our couches in front our televisions impulsively and compulsively eating because of our depression. We only add to our feelings of hopelessness while watching currently popular movie stars strut down the red carpet in fabulous dresses, most of us will only wear in our dreams. We notice how they walk, their hair, their make-up and jewelry as they pose for the cameras. Desperately trying to remember a time in our own lives when our figures possibly looked like that adds to our insecurities.

The media's constant visual stimuli convince us we are just not good enough the way we are. This conditioning not only robs us monetarily, but also lowers our self-worth and self-confidence. Notice too, the recent increase in plastic surgery. Available surgeries include nose jobs, liposuction, breast augmentations, face-lifts, eyelifts and anything else you can think of lifting can be lifted except one's true self-worth.

Every summer Caucasian female consumers spend billions of dollars trying to get brown skin, while their African American sisters spend their hard earned dollars on weaves and other hair pieces in an attempt to look like their white counterparts. We have not learned to accept ourselves or appreciate our differences. Being lured to believe we can improve our self-worth via superficial methods and with various beauty products perpetuates the masking of our inner pains and self-discontentment.

How did we become so obsessed with our outward appearance? Negative outside messages we received from the media were turned into negative internal messages. When you couple low self-esteem with the constant "perfect" images in the media, it becomes very difficult to feel good about yourself. If your family didn't instill positive approval…which most did not, where would we learn to value ourselves, appreciate our uniqueness and embrace our individuality?

This same secular world constantly reminds us we don't have enough and can't get enough. The pressure we experience in our society to keep up or stay ahead of the race can be quite overwhelming. Attempting to be the supportive wife, super mom, successful career girl, a spiritual saint and all of those other hats we wear depending on the situation can leave us feeling unquestionably challenged. You and I are all too familiar with the phrase "keeping up with the Jones's" so I won't mention them any further. What is important to realize is the "world system" wants to control our minds. Your money is the obvious objective. Marketing and advertising are the tools.

The Psychology of Marketing

Is all advertising and marketing wrong? No it is not, but because the world is successful in sales and marketing, shouldn't we discover what's at the root of its success? Though money is the goal, the force that empowers and sustains the realization of this goal is what we are after. Fortunately, we do not have to spend billions of dollars to get our results. We need only to understand the power at work behind the scenes of all advertising and marketing strategies.

Research has determined most people do emotional shopping. We are motivated to spend based on our senses.

Food advertisers appeal to our sense of sight, smell, sound, taste and touch in order to sell their products. The packaging of these products has literally become a science and is just as important as what is inside the package. Different colors produce different results, invoking different moods and feelings. Most fast food restaurants use red and yellow in their logos, on their buildings, food wrappers and drinking cups. Through research, marketing experts have determined these colors are more appealing than let's say green.

In addition to our emotional reaction to colors, another source of sense arousal is the original enticement—food. Grocery stores stock their shelves according to the products they really want to sell. More popular brands are usually at average adult eye level. Even at the check out, make no mistake, those little do-dads like razors, lighters, playing cards and candy are strategically placed there to prompt you to make another purchase. Candy is staged at children's eye level with the idea being children will plead with their parents to buy them some. It usually works. On occasion, my children have persuaded me to make purchases I had no intention of initially making.

The subtleties of worldly programming can also be found in our eating habits. Coupled with the deception of the "perfect image" is the falsehood we are not thin enough. Notice the overabundance of weight loss and diet commercials. Numerous advertisements for pills and food items are available to help us get the "perfect" bodies. It's no wonder so many of us struggle with this weight issue. Many women are on the perpetual dieting rollercoaster using unhealthy methods to lose weight—some even starving themselves to death. While countless advertisers are encouraging us to lose weight, others are simultaneously persuading us to eat more.

At the other end of the spectrum, restaurants intentionally sabotage our attempts to maintain a healthy weight. They subtly entice us to increase our food intake by serving us larger portions on larger plates. Furthermore, over the last fifteen to twenty years, fast food chains introduced us to the "biggie size", hoping we would buy more and eat more and we did. Not to be left out, the buffet-style eateries, where you can eat as much as you can eat, have lulled us into pure gluttony.

To aid us however in our battle with weight-loss or weight-maintenance, we have in recent years been introduced to new food terminologies such as, low-carb, no-carb, low-fat, reduced-fat, zero-fat and the various sugar substitutes. The manufacturers claim their products will assist us in becoming healthier and thinner, but their eventual goal is to cause us to develop a continual weight consciousness. We are literally being seduced by the food industry to be constantly concerned about our weight. With no end in sight, we don't know what they will come up with next. Food manufacturers are actually scrambling right now to determine the next diet-food fad in an effort to capitalize on our naivety, vulnerability and ignorance.

What has virtually taken place through this subtle and sometimes blatant programming is a term referred to as conditioned response. In 1904, Professor Ivan Pavlov, a physiologist and Nobel laureate, discovered through an experiment on reflexology, a behavioral reaction he termed "conditioned response". Measuring spontaneous effect was the objective of his research. His discovery was truly astounding and quite fascinating.

Using a dog, some food and a simple bell, Pavlov was able to determine certain reflexive responses to food. Each time Dr. Pavlov rang the bell, he would then feed the dog. He continued to do this over a period of time and noticed each time he rang the bell, the dog would begin to salivate and come running. After this pattern had been established in the dog's behavior, the dog had become conditioned to respond to the bell. What's notable about Pavlov's discovery, the dog started salivating every time he heard the bell regardless if food was present or not. Additionally, his findings determined the dog ate every time he heard the bell although he wasn't hungry. The dog learned to accept the bell as his signal to eat. Furthermore, the dog expected to eat because of the bell and his body reacted in accordance with his expectations. Dr. Pavlov's research concluded, given a specific set of circumstances along with the appropriate stimuli, a response could be achieved with a certain level of predictability. This is the foundation of the programming technique of the "world system".

This same conditioning is being used on innocent television viewers today, mainly through media advertisements. This is why commercials and printed media ads are so successful. The next time you are watching television, count the number of food advertisements you see. Depending on the time of day, will determine what genre of food commercials are shown. For example, breakfast food commercials are aired in the morning. Conversely, throughout the evening, you will see pizza, chicken, hamburger and various restaurant commercials. They don't have to use any catchy sound bites with the commercial because the picture alone is convincing enough for some of us to go to our kitchens to eat something. You may also find yourself from time to time compelled to pick up the phone and call for take-out by merely watching these commercials. Then some lively music, a clever jingle and a witty catch phrase is added for further sensory arousal. Some actor is then shown carefully biting into the food and we've now become so motivated to eat although we may not really be hungry. They are also careful to give us close-ups of the food, steaming hot and deliciously bathing in juices, until you can almost smell the aromas from your television set. Perhaps you are considering eating right now based solely on the last few sentences you've read. Unfortunately, our conditioned response to food advertisements has made our waistlines bigger and the fast food chain executives and restaurants owners profits larger. Wasn't food the first temptation of Eve and Jesus?

Because women usually carry the responsibility in the home for determining what the family eats, it's important to take a closer look at this role. Moms generally do the grocery shopping and prepare the meals for their families. Because of this assumed responsibility, we should make it a greater priority to become better educated about the foods we buy for our households. Additionally, with obesity on the rise amongst our children in this country, as mothers, it is imperative that we make wise decisions for our children concerning what they eat and in what quantities. Knowing what foods are healthy though has become increasingly challenging. Unfortunately, much of the food we consume is now loaded with steroids, preservatives, additives and chemicals we are unable to pronounce. It's no wonder we're having such issues with our weight and health in this current "world system".

Fairy Tales and Other Programming

We have adopted other mindsets and viewpoints from this "world system" lacking validity or credibility as well. As little girls, we were programmed to believe in "Prince Charming" or the infamous "Knight in Shining Armor" through the fairytales we read. Stories of Cinderella, Snow White and Sleeping Beauty, during our impressionable years, shaped our thinking with respect to romance and relationships. We were conditioned with the premise that someday some wonderfully, handsome man will come along, sweep us off of our feet and we would live happily ever after in his castle. Part of the problem with these fairytales is the message being conveyed to little girls; females are helpless and need to be rescued. The other issue with these seemingly harmless stories is that we are not telling our sons they are the "Prince Charmings" or "Knights in Shining Armor" expected to do the rescuing.

We should pause here for a moment and decipher "fairy tales" to get a better understanding of what and whom we've been conditioned to believe. **Fairy**— this can also be connected with the word "godmother" and is a mythical being usually thought to have magical powers. **Tale**—a lie. Upon connecting these two words, the dictionary defines fairy-tale as a made-up story usually designed to mislead.

In truth, women are conditioned to prepare for marriage and motherhood throughout their entire childhood. Not only do the stories we expose them to add to the development of this "happily-ever-after" fantasy, but the toy manufacturers contribute to our children's conditioning as well. The toys created and made available for us to purchase for our daughters are quite different than the toys manufactured for little boys. Girls are given dolls, clothes and accessories for the dolls, tea sets, plastic kitchen appliances and play houses to help perpetuate the belief in the fairy-tale ending. Boys on the other hand, are given bats, balls, trucks, cars, erector sets and play guns. What's interesting is no one has ever really challenged the toy industry to change this intentional programming of our children. Clearly differences are made in the products we can purchase for our children. While little girls are in training to become wives and mothers, our sons are taught to "just play". Boys are not afforded the same opportunity to experience relational skills development during their formative years and unfortunately reach adulthood lacking in the necessary adeptness to be successful in their roles as husbands and fathers.

In general, we have been unknowingly brainwashed by the "world system" with regards to how we respond to many of our circumstances. This is not only true where our needs and desires are concerned, but is especially true regarding our relationships. The difference between humans and Pavlov's dog though, we can choose to change our conditioning and our responses to every circumstance. By determining the thoughts and opinions adopted from the secular world contributing negatively to our well-being, further equips us to reject or reverse being conformed to this world. Learning to recognize the subtle programming of our current "world system" enables us to make better decisions. The next step is to investigate the mindsets resulting from this worldly conditioning which can cause us to behave in unhealthy ways. Moreover, understanding what we should accept and what we are expecting will aid us in accomplishing that goal.

Chapter 6

Men — Why Won't He Change?

Genesis 2:18 — And the Lord God said, "It is not good that the man should be alone; I will make him a help meet for him." **KJV**

Eve entered into a perfect world with none of the amenities, luxuries or necessities of our modern day life to concern herself with. She had no dishes to clean, no keeping of the home to tend to, no diapers to change or meals to prepare. Everything she needed had already been provided. Washing clothes and ironing were not a part of her responsibilities. Nor did Eve have the availability of shopping malls to spend her time or her money. There weren't any television shows to watch, movies to see or books to read. She only had one responsibility — be Adam's helpmeet. But just what exactly was she supposed to help Adam do?

Men need the help of a woman. God would have never called Eve Adam's "helpmeet" if that were not true. Because women were created to be a "helpmeet" it would be beneficial to dissect the word in order to understand exactly what that entails. **Help** — aid, assistance, remedy, relief, benefit. **Meet** — to become joined into one; to come together for a common purpose.

Eve was created to help Adam be fruitful and multiply. She was also created to be his companion and partner assisting him in having dominion in the earth. But as we know, her one fatal decision caused their lives to move in a direction opposite of the original plan. Soon, she discovered her role changed from being Adam's co-laborer to submitting to him. Her need to fulfill her role as helpmeet however did not change.

The distinct natural born desire to want to help our spouses, children, friends, etc is evident in all women. In fact, during the dating process prior to marriage, we'll notice what at first appear to be slight idiosyncrasies in our prospective mates. We then make little mental notes of what we purpose to change about them once we're married. Sometimes, we attempt the same strategy with our children and our friends. Actually, we are not totally wrong in our endeavor to want to help change those we care about. Our approach though, oftentimes is misguided and becomes misconstrued by the intended party. These well-intended efforts usually result or translate into nagging, whining, manipulation or control with little or no change at all in our loved ones.

Men, however do need the help a woman provides. For most men since Adam, at least one woman in his life means the world to him. Whether it is his mother, wife, sister, daughter or grandmother, men have been greatly affected and inspired by one or more of these women. During awards programs or sporting championships, you can many times hear an athlete or an entertainer at some point during their acceptance speech or an interview say, "I'd like to thank my mom" or "I'd like to thank my wife". They thank God, their managers, their fans and the like, but they seem to always include their mothers, grandmothers or their wives. Women do make a definite impact in the lives of those they care about. We sometimes however cross the line of care and concern to literally trying to change the ones we love into what we want them to be.

First and foremost, we must free ourselves from the unrealistic notion we can change another individual. Although many of us may realize this already, it can only help to reiterate this point. Much of our frustration and discontentment with our relationships would be alleviated if we would accept this fact. It's not our job to change someone else or to fix what we think is "wrong" with them. That responsibility belongs to God and the choice of change belongs to the individual. We can only hope to encourage them and be supportive.

The word "change" usually makes reference to the dying of oneself, dying to the old man or dying to the flesh. Additional definitions include implied variation; making an essential difference often amounting to a loss of original identity or to replace with another. Change then, is merely the introduction of something new into your life or the releasing of something old. When we purpose in our minds we can in fact change another person, we're deceiving ourselves and setting ourselves up for certain disappointment. We really don't want our spouses, our children or our friends to lose their original identity. They're individuality makes them unique and is what caused our love for them in the first place. We also don't want the "changee" to become someone they are unable to be for the sake of making us "happy". Change is an individual choice to be made only by the person determining they should change. We can however through prayer and discernment, discover our loved ones' potential, gifting and talents. Then, through positive reinforcement, praise and constructive suggestions, help them to become what God desires them to be.

Examine the dieter. Only the man or woman on the diet can lose the weight. I can offer support and encouragement, but until the dieter makes up their own mind to lose the weight, their weight will remain unchanged.

Change can only take place when a person makes a conscious decision after an acknowledgement and awareness that something should be added or subtracted from their lives.

Differences

Basic differences exist between men and women. Not only physically of course, but differences are apparent where our needs are concerned. Women need security and someone to listen to them. Men, on the other hand, desire praise and encouragement. Reciprocal verbal communication does not rank high on a man's list of basis needs.

When men receive praise for a job well done it strokes their egos and makes them feel needed and appreciated. My husband tickles me after he mows the lawn or tends to our flowerbeds. Sometimes after he's finished working in the yard, before I can compliment him, he'll ask me, "Doesn't my yard look good?" I have come to realize how much he needs praise. If I don't commend him in a timely manner, he's learned to compliment himself, at least when it comes to the yard. I think it's cute though and I try to make it a priority and a habit to say positive things to him. I've come to understand these basic requirements after twenty years with the same man.

In addition to positive praise, visual communication is also a distinguishing difference relative to men. The media understands this so well they feature women in advertisements to sell everything from cars, to food, to sex to...well just about anything. Furthermore, marketing majors in college are taught that sex sells. And it does, because men are usually stimulated and motivated first by what they see. Purposely many of our commercials, videos and movies are overrun with sexuality. Advertisers understand men's needs and intentionally use this knowledge when creating advertisements, music videos, movies and even game shows. Women are highly paid as visual stimulation for men to prompt them to watch. The same holds true for music videos. There again, men are the targeted audience. Shake your "derrière" and show your body and don't worry about the message being portrayed to our viewing audience. The ridiculous idea that women scantily dressed will somehow cause men to buy a particular product insults the intelligence of the viewing audience. Are men really that gullible? At least the media thinks so. Nevertheless, it sells and media advertisers repeatedly utilize this simple selling technique.

Genesis 3:6 — And when the woman saw that the tree was good for food, and that it was pleasant to the eyes, and a tree to be desired to make one wise, <u>she took of the fruit thereof, and did eat, and gave also unto her husband with</u> <u>her; and he did eat.</u> KJV

Eve is our first example of women being used as visual motivation. After Eve ate of the forbidden fruit, she doesn't say anything to Adam, rather she simply hands him the fruit and he ate also. Adam ate of the fruit without any verbal communication occurring between them. Because he *saw* her eat the fruit and appeared to still be alive without consequence, he concluded he too would be exempt from any negative repercussions. Eve's actions led Adam to sin because he was primarily visual by nature.

This too is the reason pornography is so very lucrative. Pornography is designed to be visually stimulating, mostly for men. Furthermore, movies are employing the same tactic. Rarely in R-rated or PG13 movies are men shown completely taking their clothes off. He may remove his shirt, but that's as far as it goes. While more often than not, women are filmed fully disrobing during romantic scenes. Notice the account of David and Bathsheba:

The Power of Eve

II Samuel 11:2-3 — And it came to pass in an evening tide, that David arose from off his bed, and walked upon the roof of the king's house: and from the roof he <u>saw</u> a woman washing herself; and the woman was very beautiful to look upon. And David sent and inquired after the woman. And one said, "Is not this Bathsheba, the daughter of Eliam, the wife of Uriah the Hittite?" KJV

Because David *saw* Bathsheba bathing, he lost complete control of himself to the point of adultery and murder! It's very important to comprehend just how visually stimulated and motivated men are.

Women, however are more inclined to react or become stimulated based on what they hear. As Satan appeared in the Garden of Eden, he went to Eve first. Knowing how important communication is to women, the enemy begins conversing with her. The devil concluded that if he could talk Eve into committing sin while Adam was watching, he would have them both. Eve was deceived by what she heard. Adam was tricked by what he saw.

Given that women are more aroused by what we hear, we tend to make the assumption we can use the same communicative means with men. Let's admit it ladies, we like to talk. Conversation is very stimulating for us and is one of our basic needs. Even television and radio, through talk shows, has capitalized on this seemingly insatiable need women have. On the most popular talk shows, women make up the majority of the audiences. We openly share our thoughts, feelings, interests and life stories with each other. There is nothing wrong with enjoying good, healthy conversation, but to be successful effectively communicating with men folk, we must be careful of our words and know they speak a different language.

Women, on the other hand, are usually first persuaded by what a man says, more so than what he does or how he looks. This is undoubtedly another difference between the two genders. When a man wants to attract a woman, the first few sentences out of his mouth will determine whether or not he has her attention. A man, however, will approach a woman based on how she looks, not because of her conversation. These basic differences were set in motion beginning with Adam and Eve. When God created Eve, God brought her to Adam, or better stated presented her to him. Adam, because of what he saw, immediately begins preaching and making declarations. Eve was merely listening absorbing every word.

Genesis 2:22-24 — And the rib, which the Lord God had taken from man, made he a woman, and brought her unto the man. <u>And Adam said</u>, "This is now bone of my bones, and flesh of my flesh; she shall be called Woman because she was taken out of Man. Therefore shall a man leave his father and mother, and shall cleave unto his wife, and they shall be one flesh." KJV

The Silent Communicators

While it is necessary to understand the importance of good verbal communication skills, unspoken language is part of the equation as well. What are we saying when we don't realize we are communicating? Our countenance, clothes, walk and posture communicate to those we come into contact with recurrently. I refer to these factors as **the silent communicators**. You are not audibly speaking, however messages are continuously being transmitted by one's presence, appearance and body language.

Think for a moment about the silent signals you are giving off right now. If you are getting unsolicited attention from those you are not purposely attempting to attract, you probably want to check your silent signals. The issue is not with the people attracted to you, but the messages you are conveying with body language, clothes and more importantly your conduct.

When we dress in provocative or lurid ways, more than likely we will attract unwarranted comments, looks and insults, as opposed to the compliments we may actually desire. Appearance does matter and though it does not make us who we are, it contributes to some measurable degree to silently verbalizing who we are. Furthermore, we wear these silent signals like we wear our clothes. These non-verbal ways of communicating can many times let everyone around us know what's really going on internally with us. We should determine what negative signs we are wearing and replace them with what we really want people to see. Some of the signs needing to be taken down and permanently destroyed are as follows:

I'm Desperate
I'm On the Hunt for a Husband
I'm Available
I'm Ugly
I'm Not Good Enough
I'm Not Worthy
I'm Poor/Broke
I'm A Victim
I'm Needy
I'm Insignificant

If you think you are possibly wearing one or more of these silent advertisements, consider replacing them with one or more of the following positive affirmations:

I Am Saved and Happy About It
I Am Blessed
I Am Well Able to Take Care of Myself
I Am Happily Married

I Am Fearfully and Wonderfully Made
I Am Successfully Single
I Am Victorious
I Am Significant
I Respect Myself
I Am Beautiful

Remember men are visual by nature. To effect a change in him and how he responds to you, you must be willing to change you. Situations in your life and your relationships will not change just because you want them to—you have to change. When you decide to change, others around will change. They will either adapt to your changes or you'll find new people will come into your life.

The Reality of Change

Facing reality can sometimes be very difficult, especially when it requires that we change. Confronting our issues and being honest is necessary in order to change destructive behaviors. Once I realized I didn't have to accept the way I was living and was no longer afraid of life without my husband, change for me and in me began to take place. Quite frankly, we choose to live the way we choose to live. This principle holds true for any circumstance negatively affecting or controlling your life.

Furthermore, once I made up my mind I didn't have to live with a drug addict or be one myself, was where my deliverance began. Although my husband's behavior was no longer acceptable to me, more importantly, my own behavior had become detestable and unacceptable to me! I was sick and tired of being sick and tired. I had to change me if I wanted my circumstances to change.

I had been attending church off and on for several months before my deliverance. Then, in May of 1995, I became completely free from the bondages of drugs. My husband however, was not changing and continued in his addiction. I tried everything I knew to get him to stop. I put anointing oil on his pillow, prayed and fasted, confessed Bible verses throughout the house and rebuked the devil. I cried a lot too. Nothing seemed to be working. Oh yeah, I also continuously screamed and argued with him. He just wouldn't change.

Many nights during this time I wasn't sleeping very well. I worried the police were going to come to my house with news of my husband being found dead from an overdose. Sometimes, I wished they would. I so desperately wanted something or someone to end the torment and misery I found myself in. Unable to break free from my self-inflicted prison, my husband wasn't changing no matter how much I yelled at him. I discovered through this experience that yelling does not work. Yelling and screaming only added negatively and exponentially to this dire situation. I guess I thought if I screamed loud enough he would hear me and of course change. The Bible however is clear about what happens when a woman behaves in this manner. Furthermore, Solomon gives this piece of advice twice in the same chapter of Proverbs and three different times in the same book. Perhaps one or all of his 700 wives or 300 concubines was angry, contentious and yelling.

Proverbs 21:9 & 25:24 — It is better to dwell in a corner of the housetop, than with a brawling woman in a wide house. KJV

Proverbs 21:19 — It is better to dwell in the wilderness, than with a contentious and angry woman. KJV

Because the first ten years our relationship was unstable and unhealthy, I didn't know how to deal with my husband or my emotions once I became drug-free. I literally worshipped my husband and his problem. Finally, after exhausting every possible solution *I* could think of, I fell on my knees and prayed another short prayer, "God, if you don't change him, I can't." That may not be the proper way to address God, but God knew what I meant. I continued praying, "God, if he won't change, I can't take it anymore. I can't live like this any longer God. I can't, I can't, I can't." All of those can't(s). That's exactly what God was waiting for—me to get out of the way and allow Him to do what He does best—be God.

God definitely answered my prayer. Oddly enough, I was the one God began to change first. By allowing myself to become vulnerable to God's direction, I stopped trying to change my husband and decided to change me. The first character flaw needing to be changed was my speech. It didn't take long to come to the realization I was contributing greatly to the miserable condition of my circumstances, speaking ugly words to my husband constantly. I also changed the words I spoke to others about him. This was difficult at first. Yelling and putting him down had become rather routine language for me. Boy was I an expert at this destructive behavior! Because our words have the ability to create the individual worlds we live in, we are then co-creators along with God's laws and principles of our own happiness or pain.

Finally, I realized why my husband wasn't changing. First of all, because I was speaking negative things to him constantly my words were nullifying my prayers. One day, Craig, a friend of ours abruptly corrected me as I was sounding off about my husband, "You should be more careful with your words", he said sternly. He then showed me the following scripture,

Proverbs 18:22 — "There is death and life in the power of the tongue." KJV

The Life Recovery Bible explains it this way, **"For the tongue can kill or nourish life."**

Craig suggested that I apply this scripture and see what happens. He further said I could bring about the desired outcome I was hoping to achieve if I changed what I was confessing. Soon afterwards, I started to notice a slight change in my husband once I began to say more positive things to him and about him.

Another problem I needed to address was my behavior. Not only was my conversation wrong, my attitude was as well. I was preaching Jesus and quoting scriptures, yet acting like the devil! I was letting my anger get the best of me and had become almost impossible to live with. The last challenge I had to overcome was my obsession with him. I was addicted to him and wanted so desperately to help him or perhaps "make" him change.

Needless to say, these were issues I had to come to grips with in order to see the changes I desired. I realized that though I couldn't change him, I could change me. I continued in prayer, first asking God for forgiveness for my language concerning my husband, and then asking Him to help me to better guard my words and correct my attitude.

Solomon also writes to us concerning the woman and the atmosphere of the home in another verse of scripture in Proverbs:

Proverbs 14:1 — Every wise woman buildeth her house; but the foolish plucketh it down with her hands. KJV

Clearly in this passage the onus is on the woman with regards to the atmosphere in her home. Women have the ability as wives and mothers to create homes of peace, warmth and comfort for our families or we create homes of chaos, confusion and dysfunction. Admittedly, this is something I've had to learn the hard way.

Additionally, I discovered my life and my relationships will not change just because I want them to—I have to change. Once I really started changing, the people around me started to change too. Sometimes though, when you decide to make changes for the better, those around you are not necessarily in favor of the transformation that's taking place in your life.

A few days later, I went from being broken to being threatened. One evening in September of 1995, while standing outside of my home visiting with one of my neighbors, my husband approached me to ask for some money. I refused. Unyielding to his verbal threats, he then reached out as if to grab me, never actually touching me. It was as if there was a barrier between us, preventing him from moving towards me. I stormed back into the house to call the police. Before I knew it, my husband was standing in our living room, handcuffed and heading to jail. He remained locked up for the next 37 days, just long enough for me to get a good taste of what actual peace felt like.

During this period of separation, I prayed like never before for my marriage, my husband and especially for myself. The last thing I wanted to do was become vindictive or bitter. Mostly, I asked God for peace. God moved so powerfully in my life, delivering me from my obsession of my husband as well as breaking his addiction.

Chapter 7

Awareness — Expecting What You Accept

What Is Acceptable

An important lesson I learned during this whole ordeal is **you get what you accept**. Sitting on my porch one afternoon, talking to one of my girlfriends about my marital problems, she suddenly blurted out, "You know you get what you accept. You just do, Dee." I was so stunned by the simplicity, yet in awe by the depth of what she said to me. In order for change to take place, I had to first determine what I was accepting that perhaps I shouldn't be. Although I could not change my husband's behavior, altering how I responded to him and deciding what I was willing to accept was possible.

Acceptance means giving consent or approval, and enduring without protest, the conduct or words of another individual. Negative behavior condoned and allowed rather than questioned and opposed, yields unwarranted results in our lives. In other words, we become enablers to unacceptable behavior.

Three years after my deliverance, I began counseling others with substance abuse issues. Ministering to couples dealing with this problem, I noticed a commonality. In most cases, the man was the addict and the woman the enabler. Another similarity was also prevalent—the woman had learned to accept this behavior. She had convinced herself she had to live like this and/or she was afraid of being alone. Oftentimes unknowingly, the woman actually contributes to the continued drug use. Afraid of what change will do to the relationship, she allows or accepts the man to go on living with her for more than a reasonable amount of time. It's important to note that it is not her fault he's involved with drugs. She is however to blame if she allows this behavior to persist without the both of them attempting to seek help. Unfortunately, I've witnessed couples living in this hellish condition for many years.

Mothers too, have sometimes unintentionally been a party to their own son's untimely death from drug abuse because they allowed and enabled their son's behavior. Permitted by their usually elderly mother, the adult son still lives at home. Eventually the son goes to jail or possibly prison on some drug-related charge. Once he's released, he goes back home to momma and the pattern is established. This vicious cycle persists for as long as the behavior is acceptable to the enabler.

Giving the addicted loved one money is another mistake made by well-intentioned wives, girlfriends and mothers; the idea being she's at least keeping him from committing crimes and going to prison. Unfortunately, I have been to too many funerals of drug addicts. Either the mother or the wife has, in an effort to protect and save their sons or husbands, naively hastened sending them to an early grave. This unfortunately is a harsh reality and regrettably these types of scenarios are played out over and over again in today's society. Tough love is what is needed in these situations and knowing what is acceptable is also just as important and essential.

Honestly ask yourself, what are you accepting in your life that really should be labeled as "Unacceptable"? Then don't be afraid to change it by changing you. Perhaps your circumstances are not as severe as having a husband or a child that is addicted to drugs or incarcerated, but whatever your situation is, you have the power to change your life for the better.

Expectations

Tied to the **"you get what you accept"** principle is another factor affecting our circumstances and is equally important to bring to light—**you get what you expect.** We don't expect to be abused, treated like second-class citizens, or disrespected, but truthfully we may be subconsciously bound by thoughts of low self-esteem. These inner thoughts manifest themselves in various ways. We may not say aloud, "I'm not worthy to be treated with respect", but our outward behavior let's the entire world know how we really feel about ourselves internally.

The woman being verbally or physically abused begins to slowly change her outward appearance. If she wears make-up, jewelry or goes to the beauty shop or nail salon on a regular basis, she will probably eventually stop doing all of the above. Over a period of time, her outward appearance will broadcast to the world the nature of her relationship. What she fails to realize is her decision to no longer take care of herself does not stop the abuse. In fact, not keeping her appearance up only fuels the man's loss of respect for her. He may also disallow her to take care of herself due to his loss of respect for her and his own insecurities. Either way, she is no longer as appealing to him as perhaps she once was.

This woman also begins to expect the husband or boyfriend to come home and beat her because she has now accepted him beating her. And if a considerable amount of time goes by in between "episodes" her sense of expectancy increases. The "conditioned response" principle in chapter 5 plays a major role with domestic violence as well. Accepted continual abuse is a result of conditioning.

This conditioning not only affects the wife's behavior, but it also psychologically damages the children's reality of what a normal relationship looks like. When children witness their mother being abused by their father, they will grow up to exhibit one of two behaviors based on the example they've seen. A male child will more than likely seek women that are wearing the "YOU CAN ABUSE ME" sign. If the child is a female child, she will be the one wearing the "YOU CAN ABUSE ME" sign. As adults, they will eventually find themselves in abusive relationships. Because the male child witnessed the abuse of his own mother, he also concludes women **expect** to be battered and abused.

Furthermore, the woman involved in a violent relationship fears being abused to the extent she behaves in a fearful manner, flinching and jumping every time the man moves. What develops and becomes all the more dangerous in this type of dysfunctional relationship is when the accepted behavior becomes expected behavior. Also, women who remain with men beating them or using verbal abuse as a means of control are feeding this unfavorable conduct. He beats her and she's accepted it. Then she learns to expect it. She's allowed fear's grip to convince her he'll stop. Moreover, she becomes so fearful, paralyzed by a prison having no physical bars.

If you are currently in a relationship as the one just described, you must first change what you are expecting and undeniably cease from accepting this monstrous behavior. No one should have to live like this, nor were you ordained by God to live like this. It is of utmost importance for the safety of you and your children that you seek help. Then know that you can and must get out!

Communicating Expectations

Self-esteem or lack thereof comes into play with regards to what we're expecting. Take this simple test. When someone compliments you, your response will help you to see how you really feel about yourself. For example, someone tells you, "I like your dress", or "I like your outfit". Do you respond by politely saying, "Thank you", or do you put yourself down by saying, "Oh, this old thing"? Better still, do we question the person's motive and wonder what they meant by their comment or compliment? Immediately, you have sent a negative message about what is in your heart. You don't feel good about yourself and you let everyone know it. We cannot hope to have good, healthy relationships if we are unable to receive the simplest of compliments from others. Remember, you get what you expect.

Communicating our expectations in any relationship is extremely important. However, if I don't know what I'm willing to accept or what I'm expecting, no one else will know either. I'm not necessarily referring to what you *want* from someone else, but what you expect. Once we align our expectations with God's expectations we can be assured that our results will improve. God encourages us through scripture concerning our circumstances. He has also told us what He expects. God's desire for us is to give us an expected end of peace and He really does want the best for us.

Jeremiah 29:11-12 — For I know the thoughts that I think toward you, saith the Lord, thoughts of peace, and not of evil, to give you an expected end. Then shall ye call upon me, and ye shall go and pray unto me, and I will hearken unto you. KJV

The **acceptance** and **expectation** factors are so closely related that if you determine to change one the other will change as well. I don't expect my children to embarrass me in public. If they do and they have, I immediately let them know that this is unacceptable behavior. They now know what I expect. They also know what to expect from me if they continue to behave in an unacceptable manner.

What you're expecting and what you're willing to accept is a continual process. For example, if you expect to be treated with respect you will find yourself accepting appropriate behavior from others. Should someone disrespect you, a silent alarm will go off, alerting you to the unacceptable behavior. The choice then becomes do you accept this behavior or not.

Let's say for instance, you notice during the dating process, your prospective husband doesn't open the doors for you. If you accept him not opening doors for you, then he probably won't change that particular behavior once you're married. Simply put, he doesn't see the need to change. Complaining and nagging won't change him because you initially did not make your expectations known. Men are not mind readers and usually have to have things spelled out for them. Perhaps his mother or father did not teach him it was respectful to open doors for women. The first time you dated him he didn't open any doors for you but you overlooked it and accepted it.

Making your expectations known from the beginning of a relationship will help to alleviate the need for correction in the future. Additionally, if you seem to end up on the short end of the stick with regards to your relationships, whether it's with your spouse, children or co-workers it might be time for you to reevaluate what you are expecting and what you are accepting.

Of course I want my husband to contribute to paying the bills and my children to help out around the house because it's what I'm expecting. They also expect certain things from me that I'm willing to do because it's my responsibility. If my husband stopped paying the bills just because he wanted to spend the money on himself, this would become completely unacceptable. Then the real challenge would come if what I've determined as unacceptable behavior would continue for an indefinite period of time.

When the unexpected happens, and it does, we have the ability to decide whether or not we will accept the circumstances. Sometimes situations will arise to challenge our expectations. Compromising our expectations however will lead us down the path of accepting behavior not conducive to our peace. Eve is our example of the price and the results produced when we compromise. Not only did Eve compromise, but she also lowered her standards. High standards and high expectations are necessary to bring about positive results in our respective or future relationships.

Expecting the Best

Change in our family members or in our own circumstances can happen if we believe it will. Expecting another person to change will become a reality we can anticipate only when we contribute positively through our words and actions. If our words and actions are contrary to what we're expecting and believing God for, the desired change will not come about. It is imperative for our thoughts, actions and words to be in complete agreement and alignment when it comes to the expected change. Although we may desire a particular situation to change, we may not necessarily believe it can change or will change. We also may be negating our desired results by saying the opposite of what we really want. Desire, thoughts, belief and confession must all be on one accord. You must expect the change, speak in agreement with the desired change and operate in accordance with anticipation of the change.

People will oftentimes compliment me on how sweet my daughters are. I will graciously reply with a "thank you" and agree with them. Then I will go on to explain to them my secret. From the time my daughters were born I have told them everyday that I love them. I hug them a lot too. Not only have I done these two very simple things, but I've also encouraged them to be the very best they can be. The two most important things though in raising my daughters has been my confession concerning them and my behavior towards them. My daughters *are* good and I will continue to say this about them because I know that my words carry power. I learned this lesson quite well, not only as it relates to my children but also with respect to my spouse. My positive confession and changed behavior coupled with wisdom were all major components to my husband's eventual deliverance.

The Tool of Wisdom

To aid us with becoming watchful of our words and to ensure we are speaking life into our relationships, wisdom becomes a tool of great importance. Wisdom along with prayer can equip us to make better choices and right decisions in order to avoid the traps of the adversary.

If your husband or children are not saved know they are watching you with a very critical eye. When you behave towards them in ways not conducive to them considering joining you in your faith, you will not achieve your desired results. If your unsaved loved one doesn't see you practicing what you preach you only become a hypocrite in their eyes. They see that your regular attendance at church is not changing you and therefore deduce they don't need church or God.

Husbands that are not attending church can sometimes become jealous of the church, especially of your pastor for several reasons. Firstly, the church may possibly be getting more of your time and attention than he is. Balancing your time between home and church attendance is requisite in winning him to the Lord.

Secondly, when a wife continuously reminds her husband, "The pastor said this or the pastor said that", quite frankly your husband more than likely doesn't care to hear what another man has said to his wife because he may feel somewhat threatened by your pastor's authority. Men need to feel secure about who's in charge of their home. If however, your pastor happens to be a woman, your husband doesn't really care about that either because your pastor is just another woman to him. Realize that you are your husband's primary example. He's watching you and how well you adhere to what the "pastor says".

Thirdly, you may know and even quote the scriptures in reference to how your husband should behave and what he should do. Instead of preaching to him, allowing your actions to do the preaching for you will have a much greater impact. Lastly, a wise woman will offer suggestions, sound advice or reasonable recommendations and then let it go. Driving the point home and having to have the final word will also cause your spouse to clam up and turn a deaf ear to you. It is totally a matter of choice as to whether or not your husband has heard you. Let God be God, guard your words, have a positive attitude towards him and you will see the transformation in your loved one you are expecting.

Our children and co-workers are watching us too. It becomes most important that we remember we are saved every day all day. Admittedly, this can be challenging, but for positive changes to take place keep the focus on God and yourself. Bear in mind, you get what you accept and you can expect what you're willing to accept.

Chapter 8

Witchcraft — What the Power of Eve Is Not

Before we determine what the power of Eve is, we must first find out what it is not. Demonic spiritual forces were unleashed in the earth the moment Adam and Eve ate of the forbidden fruit. These forces control and dominate our current "world system". Additionally, these same forces evident in many of our relationships today, manifest through our behavior. We may unknowingly employ these methods therefore, it is important to bring them to light.

The illusive ability Eve possessed was in no way evil. Moreover, what she had was very powerful and quite effective. This power, which is also a spirit, was created by God and given for our benefit. When this particular spirit is twisted and perverted it becomes an evil force sometimes confused with the real thing. It becomes vital then to properly identify and define the tactics, strategies and mindsets derivative of a satanic origin.

Dallas, Dee and the Devil

Ephesians 6:12 — "For we wrestle not against flesh and blood, but against principalities, against powers, against the rulers of the darkness of this world, against spiritual wickedness in high places." KJV

I'm boarding an airplane headed to Dallas to attend a telecommunications class my job required. It's early Sunday afternoon, the weather is beautiful and I'm excited about traveling again. Locating my seat on the plane, I'm grateful it's an aisle seat. After shoving my carry-on bag in the overhead compartment, I take my seat. Once we're safely in the air, the stewardess begins taking our drink orders and handing out those familiar little snacks. The man sitting next to me orders a Bloody Mary. Immediately I become somewhat agitated, silently accusing this man of committing sacrilege by wanting to drink on the Lord's Day. Almost forgetting some ten years ago, I too used to drink no matter what day of the week it was, I tell myself not to judge him.

The flight continues. Although he's a polite man, I'm still rather disturbed by his drinking. I realized though, I was not really upset with him, but I'm bothered in my spirit because of how it's affecting me—tempting me and consuming too many of my thoughts. My nose can smell the tomato juice and vodka with great clarity, differentiating between the two aromas. This man didn't know he was affecting my thoughts. He was also unaware of my former addictions. It wasn't his fault. He's innocent. I'm the target. Enticement and seduction can be so very subtle. We usually don't realize what has happened until sometime afterwards.

I managed to doze off to sleep for about one hour. The captain's voice awakens me, announcing we are experiencing slight turbulence. We are asked to fasten our seat belts. As I look around a bit, inspecting my surroundings,

I notice everyone around me is drinking some type of alcoholic beverage. To make matters worse, the man sitting next to me decides to order another drink! At this moment, my carnal mind begins to whisper to me, "You can have a drink too, Dee. No one knows you on this plane and no one will ever know. You're hundreds of miles away from home". At the same time, my spirit mind was combating every foolish thought I was thinking. "You may get away with it Dee, but God will know. You really don't want a drink anyway. You're delivered from this and will not be so easily seduced just because other people are drinking." I admit I can have some pretty bizarre conversations in my head from time to time. What could I possibly do to break this battle of thoughts in my mind, I wondered? Taking action, I picked up my pen, reached for my notebook to record this story, realizing God was trying to teach me something.

II Corinthians 10:4-5 — For the weapons of our warfare are not carnal but are mighty through God to the pulling down of strongholds; casting down imaginations and every high thing that exalteth itself against the knowledge of God, and bringing into captivity every thought to the obedience of Christ. KJV

What God showed me was just how quickly one thought can trigger a whole series of thoughts. These thoughts could eventually become an action if not properly dealt with and eliminated from the mind. Alcohol is a spirit—a spirit that used to have me bound. The devil was trying to entice me with something that would eventually cause me to feel guilty and become self-condemning. I couldn't allow the negative thoughts to take precedence over my knowledge of God's Word. God's commandments had to have the final authority over my runaway imagination. The next thing I needed to do once the wrong thoughts were arrested was to change my mind. By using writing to redirect my thoughts, I transferred what I was thinking and feeling on to my paper. This enabled me to release the thoughts from my mind and leave them in my notebook. Thankfully, through God, I was victorious that day and chalked it up to a great lesson learned about the necessity of controlling my thoughts. What I also learned from this experience is that the devil attacks a person's weaknesses not their strengths. Strongholds gain entrance and establish roots at the point of least resistance. This incident made me much more alerted to just how free flowing these negative spirits can really be.

II Corinthians 2:11 — "Lest Satan should get an advantage of us: for we are not ignorant of his devices." KJV

Careful examination of the tactics used by these demonic forces then becomes imperative for us to analyze. Manipulation, coercion, seduction and enticement are strategies used for personal gain over others and are satanic in origin. They are the perverted forms of the power that Eve possessed. Recognizing these strategies, weapons and tactics the enemy uses against us will help us to better guard ourselves from their effects.

It is our responsibility as believers to know the difference between what is true and what is not true. Only through evil suggestions can we become instruments of destructive behavior. Satan is only capable of feeding us lies when we don't know the truth or how he operates. The following relational tactics, when used by women or men, are divisive and destructive to relationships. When these methods are employed they prove unsuccessful in rendering positive results. Because the scripture is true, you reap what you sow; you cannot get positive fruit from negative seeds. Negative results will be produced in our relationships when wrong motives and tactics are utilized.

Manipulation

Manipulating someone doesn't bring about positive results because it denotes domination through words or actions that are unfair, threatening and fear inducing. Furthermore, manipulation enslaves one person to another for an indefinite period of time. When manipulative means are used to attempt to change a person, they may change, but it will not be the change we are hoping for nor will the change be permanent. Eventually, we will create a very tense and unhealthy relationship. The outcome will result in bondage for everyone involved. For example, have you ever noticed a person that seems to cause others to "walk on eggshells" just by their mere presence? Or people become fearful when that person enters the room? That's manipulation at work and is gross misuse of their position of authority.

At first glance, it appears the only person in bondage by the controlling person is the one subjected to this behavior. On the contrary, the person attempting to control another individual is also enslaved because they have a tremendous need to control others. Consequently, they do not feel as though their world is tolerable unless they are in control.

The manipulative individual is rarely a content or happy person. What they fail to understand is they can never be in complete control of their worlds and spend a considerable amount of time unsuccessfully trying to achieve this unattainable goal by means of manipulating others. The manipulator will also use guilt or condemnation as a way to control others. In some instances the manipulator plays the role of the pitiful, helpless victim in an effort to get others to feel sorry for them. They oftentimes will have you believe the rest of the world is against them, seem to always be engaged in some sort of battle or have some major problem someone else has caused for them. Manipulators using this tactic fail to take responsibility for their lives and the consequences that follow. Recall the blame game played in the garden? Adam blamed Eve and Eve told God the devil made her do it. Satan successfully manipulated both of them in order to gain control over them.

Coercion

Coercion, like manipulation, also utilizes threatening means over another person but it is more aggressive and fear inducing in its operation. Coercion includes using force or restraint to nullify and control someone's will by means of fear. Terrorism in today's society is an example of a blatant attempt to instill fear to the point of complete mental control through the use of coercion. Domestic violence is another example.

The coercive individual, for the purpose of oppression and domination, also employs intimidation. Furthermore, manipulators and coercers will generally use intimidation and violent means to mask their own insecurities. Verbal abuse and physical violence are behaviors that are prevalent characteristics of someone employing manipulation or coercion. By utilizing these two controlling operatives, the ultimate goal is to cause an individual to behave in a manner conducive to the selfish desires of the coercer or manipulator. We must conclude then, that gaining control by using these two methods over our spouses, our children or other persons will not achieve positive results. One thing is certain, when manipulation or coercion is operating in any relationship, all persons involved will become quite miserable.

Seduction

The third form of attempting to negatively control another individual is seduction. Seduction is intentionally luring someone into disobedience, thereby causing them to sin.

The person engaging in seductive measures oftentimes uses sexuality as a weapon in an effort to gain control and achieve their desired results. Results may yield temporary gratification for the seducer, but the consequences that follow can be destructive, devastating or even deadly. In an attempt to lead an individual astray, cunning persuasion and false promises are often a part of the seducer's arsenal. Moreover, the seductive personality usually comes across as charming and/or charismatic. The Apostle Paul writes to Timothy warning about seducing spirits:

I Timothy 4:1 — "Now, the Spirit speaketh expressly, that in the latter times some shall depart from the faith, giving heed to seducing spirits, and doctrines and devils." KJV

If Paul felt it necessary to address this issue with respect to the church, then we too should beware of seducing spirits in the church as well as in our personal relationships. We must also be careful that we are not the ones behaving seductively.

Enticement

Enticement like seduction is deceptive and can draw one into danger or evil by means of temptation. This particular spirit has the ability to overwhelm our senses and have a negative affect on our emotions. Enticements are presented as something to be desired or needed, and like these other demonic forces can cause a person to lose their sense of good judgment. The enticer does not necessarily use sex as a part of their arsenal, but will attempt to appeal to the sensual and emotional sides of a person. The enticer does not divulge warnings of potential danger and consequences are usually twisted into lies.

The Power of Eve

Through evoking a false sense of hope, deceptively suggesting false benefits, flatteries and instant and/or temporary gratification, the enticer can subtly accomplish their objectives. These characteristics are all a part the identifiable weaponry of this particular form of witchcraft.

We can therefore deduce that all of these spiritual forces can be dangerous and deadly. Additionally, lying and deception are rudimental ploys used by them all. That is why Satan in referred to as the father of lies. Moreover, once a person becomes seduced, enticed or tempted they can then be manipulated and consequently controlled. After Eve was enticed, she was then manipulated by Satan to subsequently entice Adam. They both became ultimately controlled by sin.

It is not necessary for woman to use seductive and enticing methods to get a man, get a job, a promotion or anything she may desire. Seduction and enticement are methods found to be evident when a woman uses pregnancy in a calculated effort to trap a man. She is also misled to believe that if I can't have all of him a part of him will do. In some instances she's also willing to share him with at least one other woman.

Men that are in this type of situation are using manipulative means to control the relationship and gain domination. He dangles his affections on a string and convinces her that no one else will want her. These methods of negative behavior unfortunately are running rampant in the world today. Women have been deceived into believing if I don't sleep with him he won't stay around. Some women even reason that perhaps pregnancy will make him stay. She may also try to give him ultimatums, which is another way she may endeavor to control him and the situation. These are all traps women sometimes attempt to utilize to "catch" a man. Understand that traps are for animals and if you set a trap you'll more than likely end up with an animal and not a man.

The Fear Factor

I Timothy 1:7 — For God hath not given us the spirit of fear; but of power, and of love and of a sound mind. KJV

Fear is an additional strategy the enemy uses to stifle progress. The spirit of fear enters through our psyche and affects our emotions. It can cause our imaginations to run wild releasing feelings of anxiety, dread, terror and panic. There are many types of fears we are all familiar with—the fear of rejection, the fear of failure, the fear of success, the fear of death, the fear of losing our jobs, the fear of divorce, the fear of illness, the fear of getting old, the fear of being alone, fear of the unknown and the list goes on.

When the spirit of fear grips your life it can rob you of your freedom. It also has the power to squelch any semblance of courage. Fear is the enemy of freedom, change, growth, potential and faith. The strange thing about fear is it can cause circumstances to look larger or worse than they really are. Perspective becomes distorted because of fear's ability to magnify situations. It's not that fear actually has any ability in and of itself but it's our imaginations, which give fear its real power.

Eve didn't know her one choice and one wrong decision due to the manipulative scheme by her enemy would result in her banishment from paradise. The consequences to follow would also bring painful childbirths and diminish her status from co-partner with her husband to him having rulership over her. She would also experience losing one son to murder and the other son to the sentence of murder. Control, enticement, seduction and manipulation by Satan were all at work to persuade Eve to commit sin against God. She had been hoodwinked and deceived by **F**alse **E**vidence **A**ppearing **R**eal. She ate the fruit because she was afraid she was missing out on something better.

Because manipulation, coercion, seduction, enticement and fear are all spirits, it's important to note their one common characteristic. They are all mind-altering spirits. Past negative experiences may open the door in our lives to these demonic forces; however, they can only gain control over us if we allow them into our minds. Take for example, the woman who has discovered that her husband is having an affair. She decides to stay in the marriage after he chooses to stop cheating. Her challenge will then be in learning to trust her husband again. The battle in her mind will ensue each time she hears him on the phone or he's late coming home from the office. Fear has gripped her mind and trust becomes difficult to reestablish. Once fear takes root, she will find herself becoming suspicious of every move he makes. Her fear will then cause her to become manipulative and controlling for the purpose of preventing having to experience any future pain caused by his past infidelity. This woman has allowed her imagined fear to dictate her behavior. She has become afraid, and understandably so, that he may cheat again and ultimately leave her for the other woman. By extending forgiveness, prayer and casting down any negative thoughts concerning her husband she can however become victorious over her fears. Additionally, her conversation must continue to line up with what God says about the situation.

I realize this is easier said than done, but know it is possible for a troubled marriage to be healed and restored. On a personal level, I have had to overcome some of these mind-altering spirits in my own life with respect to my marriage. My husband's drug addiction produced some of these same feelings and emotions in me as the woman coping with an unfaithful husband. I behaved and responded in the same manner as the woman living in an adulterous situation. If my husband said he was "just going to the store", I would watch the clock to keep track of how long he had been gone. If he came back in a reasonable amount of time and his eyes were clear, I would breathe a sigh of relief. My fears would then be dispelled. But if he didn't return home when I thought he should, I would begin to imagine all kinds of fanatical things, my nerves would be on edge and I wouldn't be able to focus on anything else.

Additionally, my husband would sneak, lie and spend hours away from home when he was heavily involved in his addiction, much like the adulterer, to cover up his whereabouts. Strange people were calling my home at all hours of the day and night. I constantly had my suspicious antennae up.

Trust in the relationship of the woman dealing with infidelity becomes damaged and my trust of my husband had been extremely affected also. Unaccounted for money was an issue too, just as it is with adultery. Though the initial cause of marital problems may differ, the resulting emotions, feelings and behaviors produced are much the same.

Should we find ourselves going through a difficult time in our relationships, taking on the wrong attitudes or mindsets can further hinder healing, restoration and reconciliation once the initial problem has begun to be corrected. Seeking appropriate counseling may also be necessary to aid in the healing process.

The Sin of Passivity

The **sin of passivity** is akin to conformity. This mindset is the enemy of responsibility, courage and our faith. Passivity will cause our lives to be controlled by the aforementioned outside forces operating in the people we have relations with and should not be an option for us. We were not born or created to be passive. When we relinquish the control and responsibility of our lives, our purpose and our destinies to someone else, we will surely become disappointed, dissatisfied and frustrated. It is not anyone else's responsibility to make us happy. Nor is it their job to ensure our peace and security. Once we relinquish the responsibility of our lives to another individual, we forfeit or give away the power of choosing what happens to us.

Operating with a passive mindset is literally accepting or enduring circumstances without any resistance. Not opting to take an active part or role in every area of our lives will surely manifest itself in a variety of ways. The woman that does nothing to end the abuse by her husband by getting out of the relationship will continue to perpetuate her own harmful condition. The wife that is living with an alcoholic husband is only enabling him thereby condoning this behavior. A mother who will not properly reprimand her unruly child will lead them down the path of destruction and may possibly at some point in time in the future find herself wondering "why" and "what went wrong".

Passivity like fear will have us living beneath our privileges and potential. The end product will be a life that is mundane and mediocre. A passive mindset will also rob us of our creativity, productivity and possibilities. Faith becomes stifled and stagnant when we are passive. Having a passive mindset is contrary to how and why God created us in that we are to be fruitful and multiply. For women this commandment was not just limited to bearing children. We should strive to be productive and fruitful in everything we do.

The Martyr Syndrome

Another mindset or attitude some women exhibit is the **martyr syndrome.** These women suffer unnecessarily because they think they are supposed to. The martyr is usually easily offended and wears their feelings on their sleeves like a badge of honor in order to manipulate others. The martyr lives in the world of denial, often blaming others for their circumstances. They also present themselves as needy and helpless. Women operating in this frame of mind appear at first to be quite emotional, but in truth they have complete control over their emotions, turning them on and off at will for the purpose of manipulating their situations.

God does allow tests in our lives from time to time, but God does not necessarily author every negative circumstance in our lives. Some of our suffering is self-inflicted. In certain instances it would be of greater benefit if we were more practical rather than spiritual. When we find ourselves in unhealthy relationships, circumstances or situations, common sense is just as important to use as spiritual warfare. Asking ourselves, "Did I cause this problem for myself", will prevent us from blaming someone else. Also, learning to ask God, "What am I supposed to learn from this test?" can free the martyr from this unhealthy mindset. God is ready, willing and waiting to give us the answers to our prayers and our dilemmas.

The Sin of Perfectionism

The **sin of perfectionism** is connected to and empowered by the need to be in control and can be a dangerous way of thinking. Spontaneity disrupts the perfectionist's plans oftentimes causing them to become frustrated. Obstacles and distractions disturb this type of person because they believe everything is supposed to go smoothly all of the time. We are not perfect creatures but we are being perfected. Being perfected is allowing God to make us whole or complete— not perfect.

In the beginning of Eve's life she had the perfect life. She was created as the perfect companion, the perfect woman, the perfect mother. Satan's scheme was to completely disrupt and destroy Eve's perfect world and kill God's perfect creation. Because Eve failed to understand that she was already complete and perfect in the eyes of God she made a very costly mistake.

I've battled with perfectionism for a long time until one day I realized that I was missing out on enjoying my life. Working in the computer field most of my adult life only added fuel to my perfectionist ways. In the world of computer science, programs, configurations and ip addresses have to be exactly right or they don't work. It had to be perfect. The mindset I had to have for my job spilled over into the way I viewed my life.

When my first marriage fell apart I was only 25 years old. I hadn't done very many things right for about six years prior and I was having a very difficult time transitioning into adulthood. My perfect fairytale ideals about how my life was supposed to play out contradicted my reality. When my perfect world fell apart, I did too. I gave up trying to be perfect and became rebellious and depressed instead. Depression is what led me down the path of self-destruction, turning to drugs and alcohol to escape. I rationalized that if I couldn't do anything right (be perfect) I would become the best failure I could possibly be.

After my deliverance from my addictive lifestyle, I found myself once again operating with a perfectionist mentality. The more perfect I tried to become the more I was left feeling frustrated most of the time. I fell into the "if only" trap. If only I could lose 20 pounds, if only I could pray more, if only my finances were in perfect order, if only I could get my children to stop leaving things all over the house, if only I had graduated from college, if only I had more time then my life would be perfect! I was like a dog chasing its tail, never being satisfied or grateful for the day I had been given. This recording played over and over in my mind like a broken record. The perfectionist mindset was robbing my peace and the joy of being saved. Mistakenly, I translated being saved into having to be perfect.

My oldest daughter's words to me some years ago rescued me from this way of thinking. One morning as I was fussing about clothing and other items lying around the house out of place, she said in a calm but correcting voice, "Ma, you have kids. Your house will not be perfect." I reluctantly stopped complaining and came to appreciate her wisdom. I have to admit though, that I still prefer things to be in order, I just don't get stressed out about it anymore if they're not. There is nothing wrong with wanting our homes or lives to be in order, but when we cross the line to the point of obsession, we will find ourselves committing **the sin of perfectionism.**

The Silent Treatment

Silence is golden, but not when it's used to control or manipulate another individual. Both men and women alike have used this ploy. When we shut down and cease from talking we are still, however, communicating. The old adage "actions speak louder than words" is more than just a quote. What happens almost automatically when we stop communicating with one another is the mind goes into the realm of assumption. **The silent treatment** causes our imaginations to begin to wonder off in the wrong direction and our perspective of situations and circumstances becomes distorted. This tactic, like the others listed will only bring about further division in a relationship. It's best to keep the lines of communication open and choose your words wisely.

Though Satan's forces are at work, we are now able to recognize these demonic spirits and disarm them. By acknowledging improper and unhealthy mindsets we can make the decision to change them. It's also necessary for us to determine what we will accept and what we are expecting. Furthermore, taking charge of our thoughts and actions will bring deliverance and healing to our relationships. And finally, in order to live victoriously we must now discover the power that Eve possessed.

Chapter 9

The Revelation — What Eve Was Given

I have read the story of Adam and Eve many times and have heard it told from the time I was a child going to Sunday school. I had never seen this revelation before until one Saturday morning while studying my Bible I decided to ask God one simple question. Why Eve? More specifically, why did Eve eat of the tree of knowledge of good and evil first? Many preachers teach that Adam fell and blame him for sin entering into the world. But we all know it was Eve who initiated "the fall". She persuaded Adam and was the reason for their demise. Why then, because I am a woman, a descendent of Eve, do I have this horrible feeling of being somewhat to blame for the ills of humankind? Why God, why?

My thoughts and questions continued in an almost childlike manner...and God why did I become freed from my addiction five months before my husband received his deliverance? He was supposed to be the head of the household; he was supposed to be the leader and the forerunner in my home, I reasoned. Shouldn't my husband have gotten free first and then I would surely have followed him? This just didn't line up with what I had been taught about the hierarchy and the order of God concerning the family. God is head of man and the man is the head of the woman. Why did I get clean first... God please tell me why? Ending my queries to God with one last question...and why did Satan target Eve instead of going straight for the jugular, which was Adam?

After some time of intensely pondering all of these questions, God in a soft, calm voice said to me, "Eve had **influence** and Satan knew it." I responded loudly with, "Oh my God!" I slammed my Bible shut as if in disbelief of what I had just heard. My mind began to race because the answer not only unlocked the secret to what happened in the Garden of Eden, but it also provided the answers to what had taken place in my life. I reopened my Bible to read the story again. It made so much sense. Satan used Eve, being the weaker vessel only in strength, but the stronger vessel with respect to influencing Adam.

I could hardly contain myself. The answer was so clear to me especially in retrospect of my own deliverance. I reached for my dictionary next to find out exactly what influence meant. Overwhelmed with amazement, I immediately shared this revelation with my middle daughter. After I told her what God had spoken to me, all she could say was, "Wow!" I knew I was on to something and was only beginning to absorb what God had revealed to me. From that moment on my life has changed. I've come to realize my influence not only with my husband, but also with others is quite powerful.

Influence is not just a descriptive word it is also a spirit. It is mysteriously intangible and can seem somewhat illusive because it originates from the ethereal or heavenly realm. As a spiritual force sent to us from the heavens, it is continuously free flowing. Because of this fact, influence is always readily available to us. Furthermore, the ethereal or heavenly realm is as far as we can imagine. At the same time it's as close as we realize it is. There is no line of separation between the ethereal (spiritual/heavenly) or physical (natural/

earthly) realms. Webster's definition gives us further clarity: **Influence — an ethereal fluid thought to flow from the heavens and affect the actions of man; the act or power of producing an effect or a change without apparent exertion of force or direct exercise of command; to have an effect on the condition or development of.** Another way of explaining this definition is when words are paralleled with a corresponding action, those around us will respond and ultimately react to what they are hearing us say and seeing us do. Influence is powerful stuff!

Shortly before I was completely delivered, I was sharing my thoughts and feelings with another one of my friends. I had stopped using drugs five months earlier. This was now September 1995. I was telling her I wanted to leave my husband because I didn't want to continue living the way I was living. Gaining my freedom from him was imperative because he didn't seem to want to let go of his addiction. My life was in utter turmoil and it was more than obvious to me he was only contributing to making it worse. I further explained to her if I left him, I could start over again and surely live a better life without him. You know the old cliché "I can do badly by myself". But my girlfriend disagreed with my decision and told me I held the key to my marriage staying in tact. She said, "Don't you know he loves you and will follow you anywhere?" I didn't want to hear or believe what she was telling me at the time because I didn't quite fully understand what she was saying. I didn't want him to follow me. I was supposed to be following him and that wasn't working.

After God whispered the mystery of Eve's power to me and I understood the definition of influence, I realized what had taken place in my own life. The question that had plagued me, "why was I delivered first", was now answered. Prior to my husband's deliverance, I didn't understand just how visually oriented he was or how influential I could be.

But when I began walking in my deliverance, God used me as an example to my husband to *show* him it could be done. Once he *saw* I had really changed, he would either have to change or risk losing me. I didn't have to give him any ultimatums because he was no longer comfortable with being around me while he was high. Light and darkness cannot coexist. Nor could I tolerate the spirits that had him bound any longer. I knew that my husband wanted so desperately to be free, but he didn't know how to do it. I am thankful to God for using me in this way.

This transformation in our lives particularly early on however was not easy. I had to practice tough love and become selfish about my own life and deliverance as well as my children's wellbeing. I determined that with or without him I was going to change my life. The night after he had been taken to jail, I remember falling on my face, praying to God, "If I have to live without my husband, I'm willing to do so for the sake of serving you and for my own sanity." The next morning, I went downtown to the courthouse, filed a restraining order and pressed charges against him while he was in jail. This was one of the most difficult things I've ever had to do. I felt so alone, but determined all the same. At the time I was working a job that only paid minimum wage and didn't know how I was going to survive—$1000 a month doesn't go very far with 3 children to take care of.

During those thirty-seven days while my husband was in the local jail, waiting for his day in court, I prayed vehemently to God to take any form of malice and vindictiveness out of my heart. Everyday I asked God for peace in my mind and in my home. I told God I forgave my husband for every thing that had happened. I still loved him and didn't want anything more for him than his deliverance. Knowing the sincerity of my heart, God answered my prayers.

The day that I went to court the district attorney approached me and asked me what I wanted to do. I told him that I just wanted my peace. My husband was supposed to spend 120 days in jail, but the judge decided to release him after I had spoken with the DA. My husband was released and we were reunited a few days later. I knew I was taking a big chance allowing him back into my life, but I believed God had delivered him. Our lives began to change dramatically. I know I was able to witness my husband's brokenness and his deliverance because I had decided to change. I was also no longer willing to accept his addictive lifestyle and made my expectations very clear.

When God answered my question as to why I was delivered before my husband this next passage of scripture helped me to understand what had really taken place.

I Peter 3:1-2 — "Likewise, ye wives, be in subjection to your own husbands; that if any (husbands) obey not the word, they (husbands) also may without the word be won by the conversation of the wives. While they (husbands) behold your (wives) chaste conversation coupled with fear." KJV

This scripture helps us to realize that we have the ability and power to win even unsaved husbands! Your influence is the key which simply stated is *godly conversation + godly conduct = saved husband*. Further study of this scripture reveals to us that the word *conversation* translated from the Greek is *conduct*. When you combine godly conversation with godly conduct your husband will receive Christ and be transformed before your very eyes.

How can we be so sure? God has proven His faithfulness to this promise through my own testimony. I've also seen this transformation take place in the lives of other couples that I've known. Those of you that are reading this book and your husband is not saved, I've hopefully assisted you in understanding that it is possible for him to receive salvation and you hold the key! You are not, however, your husband's savior. Only Jesus Christ can save him. You do have the ability though, to influence him in the right direction. I must also interject, if you are currently dating a man with the anticipation of marriage and he is not saved this scripture does not apply. We don't want to have to convert him after marriage. I know this may sound elementary, but because women have the ability to be quite influential, we will overstep our boundaries if we attempt to become his savior. Pray for his salvation prior to marrying him.

You may perhaps be assigned to your husband's life to lead him back to God as I was, but God never instructed me to save him. It's important as wives to discern where our help ends and God's intervention begins. The only help God needs from us is to be an example of godly behavior and to be careful with our words.

As we discovered in the previous chapter, influence is not manipulation, enticement, coercion or seduction. Those strategies are used by Satan and are the perverted forms of influential power. Neither is it solely the power of suggestion, because suggestion is only effective through audible communication and doesn't necessarily have a corresponding action associated with it. Influence is much more than that. It couples communication and action together to create a powerful force and brings about a change. Unlike conditioned response where repetition is its key ingredient, influence is not always contingent upon repetitive actions or constant verbalization of the same request.

Influence is what assists our faith and determines our actions although results are not always automatic. Sometimes its affects are not noticeable until some time later. Positive conversation as well as consistent godly conduct contributed to the change in my husband's life. Trusting God would change him as I walked in agreement with what God was doing through me was vital. For those who utilize the principles of this God-ordained power, you will witness change in your lives and in your relationships too.

All women have the power of influence and the power to influence. We were born with this tremendous ability, but because of the lies of the devil we've either forgotten we have it or don't realize we do. Hurtful relationships, continuous negative and erroneous media stimuli, shattered dreams and lost hopes have diminished our influential ability. Overindulgences of our flesh and the busyness of life have distracted us from being the influential people we could potentially be.

This is what Satan was actually after that day in the "garden". The devil knew Eve had influence so great she could cause Adam to sin against almighty God! Once Adam *saw* Eve did not immediately die from eating the forbidden fruit, he thought it would be safe for him to eat of the fruit as well. Satan also knew if I became delivered from the bondages of substance abuse, my husband would surely gain his freedom too. When my girlfriend told me if I got myself together my husband would follow me, I didn't think she knew what she was talking about. But she understood something I did not—**the power of influence**.

Even the secular world has clued us in through countless love songs, memorable poetry and numerous clichés that let's us know there is something to be said of a woman's influential power. Consider Percy Sledge's timeless ballad "When a Man Loves a Woman". This song has some pretty powerful and interesting lyrics.

> When a man loves a woman can't keep his mind on nothing else.
> He'll change the world for the good thing he's found.
> If she is bad he can't see it. She can do no wrong.
> He'll turn his back on his best friend if he puts her down.

When a man loves a woman, spend his very last dime.
Trying to hold on to what he needs.
He'll give up all his comforts and sleep out in the rain
If she says that's the way it ought to be.

Consider also just how impressively accurate these next three clichés are. We quote them in a kind of casual way and sometimes perhaps even jokingly, but there is tremendous truth in these statements and influence is the operating factor:

"If momma ain't happy — nobody's happy."

"Beside every great man is a great woman."

"Happy wife, happy life."

Influence is a special gift from God that we were all born with. For women, it's what puts the "help" in helpmeet. Men also have an influential ability however a man's influence is founded in his authority, masculinity and in the deepness of his voice. A woman's femininity, softness and elegance are the distinguishing features as to how she activates hers. There is no greater characteristic that enhances a woman's beauty than the power God gave Eve. I'm not referring to sexuality in the way the media portrays and exploits women...I'm speaking of the sensitive nurturing nature women possess. Furthermore, the utilization of godly influence must be taken very seriously. It is a power and key ingredient given to women to assist us in being successful in our relationships. It should not be used casually because it is a power and a spirit with energy that is continually moving and progressing.

Influence With vs. Influence Over

Influence has the ability to work in both directions—to the negative or to the positive. What's more it is the operating force behind every advertising campaign and marketing strategy. Although the media will try to convince us they are not responsible for the actions of the general public, they do in many instances attempt to gain influence over us. They understand quite well that women possess a special kind of influence and because of this attribute we are used to sell any and everything. The strategies that the "world system" uses, however, are the manipulative, seductive and enticing forms of influence and oftentimes exploits the very essence of women's femininity and dignity.

We must be very careful to not only guard our eyes and ears from negative influences, but also learn to recognize when we are being negatively influenced. Seductive influence is what sells sex and pornography. The enticing form of influence is what persuades us to eat more than we should. Coercive influence is what causes domestic violence and wars while manipulative influence is what makes drunk drivers kill. It was that same manipulative spirit that tempted me that day during my flight to Dallas. Even laws governing drinking and driving determines a person that drinks and drives is "Driving while Under the Influence".

There is a difference between our having influence with someone as opposed to having influence over someone. Our goal should always be to effect a positive change. If we focus on being the best person we can be, adhering to high standards for ourselves, those around us and especially closest to us will be positively affected for the greater good of the relationship.

When someone is described as being "influential" it's usually used in a favorable light. It's a person that is to be admired, respected and has influence **with** others. If this same individual is operating in one of the perverted forms of influence you will hear said of them, "He or she is a bad influence." In other words they are probably a manipulative, enticing, seductive or controlling person and are seeking to gain influence **over** others.

Moreover, we don't want to have or attempt to gain influence over someone as that denotes one is superior to the other. A healthy relationship should never have its foundation rooted in any form of dominance. Although the man is the head of the woman, she can be effective in her role as the helpmeet and he in his role as the head when both understand that they are to be submitted to each other first. In the epistle of Ephesians this next verse of scripture was written for both the husband and the wife to adhere to:

Ephesians 5:21 — Submit yourselves one to another in the fear of God. KJV

One additional component is vital though to successfully activating your influence. You must use the eyes of your faith to enable you to see your unsaved loved one as God sees them. This can be quite challenging at times but it is absolutely possible to achieve. Ask God through prayer to show you your spouse, child or other family member saved and delivered. You must have a clear picture in your mind and in your spirit of God's image of them and not your own. You will then through faith be able to see them already saved and delivered. As stated previously, we can't change others we can only influence them to change by our encouragement and example.

Remember influence is not enticement, manipulation or seduction. **It is the act or power of producing an effect without apparent exertion of force or direct exercise of command.** Better stated, influence is the ability to motivate someone to change from within. In order to motivate someone in a positive direction there must first be a reason, need, motive or desire. Eve did not have to force Adam to eat of the fruit. All she had to do was show him the results. I too, did not have to throw tantrums about my husband's substance abuse. All I did solely through the power of God and with my influence was show him the benefits of abstaining from what had had us so bound. Additionally, there are contributing factors that caused this change to take place. By exploring these factors we will gain understanding of how our influence can successfully produce our desired results.

Chapter 10

Factors — How It Works

With every spiritual gift, accompanying principles and factors contribute to the level of power and successful operation of its use. The governing factors, which facilitate and control the functioning of our potential influential ability are necessary to explore for further empowerment. Understanding the principles and factors connected with the spirit of influence will bring about success in our relationships as a result of its proper use. Careful application of these descriptive characteristics or factors increases the effectiveness of our influence.

Laws must be obeyed in both the spiritual and natural realms to avoid unwanted consequences. Furthermore, without laws we would live in utter chaos. God, through His infinite wisdom ordained laws and principles for us to abide by. When God established the laws, they were not given to put us in bondage, but just the opposite, to make us free.

Let's take the example of marriage. The foundation of a successful marriage is possible through the operation of the spirit of love. Some of the characteristics exhibited when love is in operation are caring, patience, giving, selflessness, forgiveness and faith. Believing your marriage will be blessed is the first step and is where faith becomes activated and is exercised. The next step is to operate in the spirit of love, applying the principles of giving, patience and forgiveness. The governing law of sowing and reaping, the third step, will automatically produce the results of a blessed and happy marriage through the vehicle of faith and the spirit of love. Faith and love working together accomplish the plan of God for a successful marriage.

As love and faith are both action words, so it is with influence. Influence, like faith and love is also immeasurable. Only you can determine how much or how little you have. Consequently, seven basis factors govern the amount and level of influence you can potentially possess. Influence can be altered, strengthened, and maintained by the following seven factors: Relationship; Trust; Perception; Attitude; Responsibility; Decisions; and Money.

The Relationship Factor

We should first take into consideration the composition of our various relationships, as it will help us to determine those we are influenced by and are able to have influence with. The opportunity to be positively influential continuously presents itself within our families, on our jobs, at church, at school or practically anywhere else we may go. This is what is referred to as your *sphere of influence*. Identifying and understanding our role in each of our particular relationships further assists us in realizing the amount of influence we possess within our sphere of influence. For example, a pastor has a greater level of influence because of the weight of the responsibility of their position or title coupled with the number of people they come into contact with. This is just one example of **the relationship factor.** The same is true for others in positions of leadership. It becomes imperative then, for persons of authority and/or leadership to use their influential ability *with* and not manipulative means *over* the people they are leading.

Deception, intimidation and manipulation are the enemies to an influential leader. The ability to positively affect those being led will seriously diminish and probably result in resentment towards the leader should these methods be employed. Pastors, managers, politicians, doctors, teachers and parents, to name a few, should pay particular attention to persons in their sphere of influence and use their ability to influence others wisely.

Those of us privileged to parent should realize our children are quite impressionable and innocently trusting. Because this is true, parents are the most influential people in a child's life. It not only matters what we say but more importantly what we do, especially where children are concerned. Additionally, we have a tremendous amount of influence with our children whether we are trying to or not.

I remember the first time my mother visited my home after I was married. While noticing my kitchen, she became somewhat amused. Her attention was directed toward my dishes and other kitchen items in my cabinets and their particular locations. Pots, pans, silverware and glasses were all positioned as if she had put them there herself. My mother didn't know until that moment she had had that kind of an impact on me. In our relationships it's important to keep in mind that our influence will not always be immediately apparent.

Because the relationship between a husband and wife is like none other, it should be cherished, appreciated and nourished. As wives, our influence with our husbands can be motivational as well as inspirational. Historically, men have been inspired throughout the ages by women. We see this fact evidenced clearly in the arts, athletics and entertainment world. When inspired by a woman there is nothing a man is not able to accomplish. Furthermore, women have an indisputable ability to build a man up or tear him down. The spirit of influence is undeniably at the root of a man's inspiration and the driving force behind his motivation.

Another aspect of the relationship factor is popularity, which can cause our level of influence to increase as well. Though we need not seek popularity as goal to be attained, it will become automatic as our sphere of influence grows. Who we know, in addition to who knows us, is important to give adherence to with regards to the relationship factor. Because of their visibility and popularity in the public sector, entertainers, athletes, politicians, clergy and the wealthy have a greater opportunity to influence more people. Influence can therefore be far reaching based on not only our relationships but trust also plays an important part of this equation.

The Trust Factor

This factor is of great significance in determining one's influential level. Honesty is the primary foundation of **the trust factor**. Trust is increased and credibility is strengthened where honesty is found. Honesty assuredly enhances influential ability. Do what you say you'll do and keep your word.

The trustworthy person is a person of integrity and reliability. Being reliable or dependable increases trust all the more, which will in turn increase our influence. Furthermore, trust is predicated upon the character of an individual, therefore character is also an essential ingredient in the trust factor. Character plays quite a major part of this particular principle because it speaks of an individual's ethics and moral values.

Godly morals and values are of immense importance to the trustworthy individual. To the influencer trust is a precious commodity. They understand once trust is damaged it is difficult to restore. A relationship in which the trust has been broken lessens or possibly destroys one's ability to positively influence the person that was hurt. Only time and forgiveness can mend and restore a relationship where trust has been violated.

Sometimes though, trust is extended without first determining credibility of character. This can be detrimental to us. Eve appears to have trusted Satan to some degree. She didn't perceive him properly thus relinquished her trust to him. By trusting in the wrong thing or person we can become easily influenced toward making the wrong decisions. Perception now comes into play and is the third influential factor.

The Perception Factor

The extent to which we can influence or be influenced will be contingent upon discernment through **the perception factor**. Perception has its foundation based on how we see others and situations. We either see the glass as half empty or half full. Through the perception factor the viewpoints and opinions we hold of ourselves, others and our worlds produce positive or negative results.

Perception then is the ability to look further than the natural eye. During the process of perception observation is made, insight is gathered and a conclusion is drawn. Consequences as well are weighed out during this process. And because perception is determined through our intuition or the senses, it can become distorted when we don't accurately see situations or people for what or who they truly are. On the other hand, when we perceive others or situations properly, we will make the right choices or decisions thereby enhancing our influential ability. To assist us with having better perception, discernment and sound judgment are necessary components to utilize. Unfortunately, Eve appears to use neither.

Because Eve was Adam's wife and his helpmate, he trusted her even though he knew she had made a wrong decision. Adam concluded that Eve could be trusted because she was a gift from God. Prior to Eve eating of the forbidden fruit, Adam had no reason to doubt her trustworthiness, and understandably so because everything God had given Adam prior to Eve's beguilement and subsequent sin had been good for him, including Eve.

The factors of perception, trust and relationship where Eve is concerned are necessary for us to further investigate. Eve had had no previous relationship with the serpent and unfortunately misperceived who Satan was. Misperception causes confusion and misunderstanding in our relationships. Eve believed the serpent though he was dishonest and surrendered at least some level of trust to him. When perception is distorted as in the case of Eve, it will oftentimes lead to wrong decisions, which will then affect the level to which we can be influential. False assumptions and drawing the wrong conclusions are directly related to having misperceived someone or some set of circumstances. To avoid being misperceived making our expectations known and clear is essential.

Effective communication will therefore enhance our desire to be correctly perceived and is vital where our relationships are concerned. The tone of our voice, the choice of our words, our appearance and our behavior all affect how we are perceived. When someone meets you for the first time they see you before they hear you. This is where the silent signals we are giving off can help us or hurt us with respect to being positively influential. Body language and/or our actions as well as verbal communication collaboratively send messages to those around us, affecting their perception of us. With this being the case, attitude is the next factor we want to closely examine.

The Attitude Factor

We have all heard, 'your attitude determines your altitude', but our attitude also determines one's ability to positively influence those within the sphere of influence. **The attitude factor** refers to and is reflective of one's mental state. Your mental state controls your emotions and sends signals to those around you as to how you are really feeling. This too is where our countenance, conversation, posture and clothing all play a vital role in strengthening and increasing our level of influence.

Influential people are not perfect people they have just learned how to maintain a positive attitude. A positive attitude is like a magnetic force that draws people to us. When you feel good about yourself, you will hold your head up and your walk will be that of confidence. Moreover, your outward appearance will send the message to others that you have an optimistic attitude. Smiling, being polite and having good manners are also quite beneficial to being influential, especially to those closest to us.

On the other hand, self-condemnation is an enemy to maintaining a positive attitude. This frame of mind is something we all battle with at times and is one of the manifestations of a negative mindset. It also damages our ability to positively affect our surroundings. Again, take time to think about what you are thinking about. We will all from time to time make mistakes or say something wrong. Self-condemnation will try to creep in to our thoughts. One of the best ways to combat beating yourself up is to find humor in your mistakes. You may also ask yourself, "What could I have done differently?" This is a good way to avoid making the same mistake again. Another combative measure is forgiving oneself or someone else and then letting it go. If an apology to someone is warranted in a given situation, apologize and move on. Taking responsibility for and admitting where we were wrong goes a long way in maintaining one's level of influence with others.

A bad or negative attitude repels people. For the influential person, there is no room for complaint or pessimism. A depressed attitude can also affect our sense of responsibility. We may only give half of ourselves to our relationships and responsibilities because we don't have a positive outlook. This downbeat attitude may stem from past hurtful experiences. Learn to shake off all negativity. Time is precious and life is short. Make the decision to live with a positive mindset and watch your life change and your influence grow.

The Responsibility Factor

Influence is further enhanced through initiative because initiative is the introductory step to **the responsibility factor**. Taking the initiative will cause our responsibilities to increase which will also raise our level of influence and expand our sphere of influence. Usually when someone takes the initiative to change something about themselves those that are around them will become influenced by the behavior that is altered. Initiative then, is the act of making the first step or the first move based on our sense of responsibility in a given situation. The importance of taking the initiative to invoke a positive change of a particular circumstance finds validation in the Biblical principle of sowing and reaping. Taking the first step, for example with your spouse is where the sowing takes place. The way that he reacts or responds to you is where the reaping is realized based on the seeds you've sown. This is why it's extremely important that we sow good seeds towards others, especially those we love and live with. Every reaction whether positive or negative can be traced back to a seed that was sown.

I can sometimes go for weeks without cleaning my house. (Not something I'm proud of). My husband, thankfully, has never complained about my tendency to neglect some of my household chores. What is interesting though is that as soon as I begin cleaning, my husband and children fall in line like soldiers pitching in until the house is once again spotless. I don't have to yell, or beg, or say anything, they just do it. All I have done is taken the initiative because I am responsible for keeping my home clean. My family then feels compelled to help me. I've also noticed that none of them will take the initiative and begin cleaning on their own. They don't feel the weight of the responsibility like I do. This same "lead by example" technique unfortunately does not work where the dishes are concerned, but I have found it to work with the laundry. I'm certain that it's because they've deemed the laundry more valuable because some of the clothes belongs to them. Whereas the dishes are "mine" therefore they don't feel ownership or responsibility.

We must also be able to differentiate between what we are responsible for and who we are responsible to. I am responsible **for** my children until they become of age. I am also responsible for my bills and my possessions. On the other hand, I am responsible **to** my husband, my friends and my pastor. And though I am responsible to my employer, I am responsible for my job. When we neglect or step away from what we are responsible for or who we are responsible to, what we are doing in effect is hindering or possibly negating our influence and stifling our true potential. Making excuses in an effort to justify being irresponsible is damaging to the objective of becoming an influencer. Balance and boundaries however are key and necessary. We don't want to overextend ourselves feeling as though we are responsible for everything and everybody. An influential person delegates certain responsibilities because it assists them in getting more accomplished. When we achieve our goals our attitude and how we feel about ourselves improves. We will feel better, it will show in our countenance, we will make better decisions and our influence will ultimately increase.

The Decision Factor

The decision factor can help or hurt the level of influence we possess. When we make a wrong decision our influence with others is affected. Depending on the severity of the effects of the bad or wrong decision, the results produced will be in direct correlation with the choice that was made. This is where introspection plays an important role in the decision factor. When we look at the choices we make on a daily basis we can determine that many of our choices are the same day in and day out. These choices then are what determine our habits and establish patterns or paradigms in our lives.

The first part of the process in **the decision factor** is determining whether this is a situation that I can influence towards change. Count up the cost and pray for wisdom. Some battles are just not worth fighting. For example, when a woman finds herself in an abusive relationship she usually sees the signs of an obsessive personality in the man before he ever lays a hand upon her. This type of man generally has a very dominant, controlling personality. He tends to be demonstrative and intimidating but because he tells her he loves her she chooses to believe his words rather than his actions. Instead of trusting her gut instincts or her spirit, she follows her flesh, while convincing herself that she is following her heart. In this type of situation, our flesh will always cause us to make the wrong decision, therefore we should pray for guidance to help us make the right decisions.

It is always wise to go to God before making life-altering decisions. Examples of life-changing decisions are marriage, schooling, childbearing, jobs and relocations. We should also consult God and seek godly counsel before we end a relationship, especially marriage. Some situations though are obvious. If your husband is physically abusive, by all means get the necessary help and then get out!

When we make the decision and choose to believe one of Satan's lies, we wind up like Eve in bondage. The result of Eve's one decision was not only tragic for her family but for all families yet to come. She unfortunately was unaware of the magnitude of the destructive results her **one** decision that **one** day would cause.

Another very important life lesson we can learn from Eve is that one seemingly small selfish decision can wreak havoc in our lives for the rest of our lives and damage our influence. If we look even closer at **the decision factor** it only takes one day to make one decision to completely change our future. It only took one decision and one day for me to get saved; one decision and one day to get married; one decision and one day to become pregnant; one decision and one day to have a baby; one decision and one day to buy a house and so on. And though each of these decisions only took one day to make, each of them have had a lifelong effect.

I only needed to say "yes" one time to cocaine to begin a life of self-destructive behavior. Another "yes" to heroine three years later continued this pattern. What I didn't understand were the consequences of these decisions until they had fully manifested in my life. One decision one day to use drugs left me penniless, homeless, unemployed and very desperate. How could I have known that one decision to have what I thought was "fun" would be so costly? But isn't that just like Satan's devices? He can dress things up in the prettiest of packages just long enough for us to become trapped.

Likewise, it only took one day and one decision on my part to shift the paradigm and stop using drugs. That same determination for a better life and choosing to change is what assisted me with making better decisions. Today, through my testimony, I can influence and encourage others that are struggling with addictions to obtain their freedom from the bondages of self-destructive behavior.

Money Is Important, But Not Necessary

We have probably all heard of the cliché, "money talks", and it does. Money has its own powerful ability to influence our attitudes and actions. And because of this truth the person that has a lot of it also can potentially have a great deal of influential power. Though money has its place, it's not necessary to have riches in order to be influential. Teachers are some of the most influential people there are, but they don't usually make a lot of money. Pastors and parents as well are quite instrumental in our lives and possess a tremendous amount of influence, yet they may not be wealthy. Conversely, a person may have great sums of money, but very little influence if they live in reclusion or have publicly made bad decisions.

Matthew 6:21 — For where your treasure is there your heart will be also. KJV

Jesus taught that money has the ability to influence our thoughts because it is closely tied to our heart. People in general are emotional about their money. It's not that money has any real power in and of itself, but we have given it influential power over our feelings to the extent that it can control our attitude and decisions. Notice how much happier people are on payday or at the first of the month. Conversely, when a person has no money or has money problems they tend to be depressed.

Sometimes money is used to try to control and manipulate others especially in relationships or on jobs. Countless people in our society are in jobs they really don't want or enjoy only because of the money they're being paid. And many people have done things they've lived to regret all because of money's influential power.

We may sometimes spend money to purchase things we don't really need or can't afford in an attempt to feel better. Using money in this way usually has an adverse affect on our relationships. Marriages have oftentimes ended in divorce because of money issues. Friendships as well can be destroyed for the same reason.

Advertisers know that people oftentimes shop based on their emotions. This is another reason commercials are aired so frequently and enormous marketing budgets are set aside by companies to advertise their products. Getting your money is the goal and influence is the key factor used by advertisers to achieve that goal. If they can arouse or stimulate your feelings about a particular product you are more likely to buy it.

Women are especially targeted in shopping malls because we tend to be more emotionally expressive than men. The next time you visit your local mall, count the number of women's clothing and shoe stores verses the number of men's shops. There are on average three times as many stores available for women as there are for men. I'm not at all inferring that shopping, spending money or having money is sinful or wrong, but understanding the power money has is important so we are not controlled by it. We should have money, but money should never have us.

Money is a tool used to sustain and enhance our lives. Know that God wants to bless us in all areas of our lives including our finances. Therefore, good money management is essential to strengthening our influential ability. The enemy knows that if we get a handle on our money we will ultimately have greater influential power. This is why Satan continuously wars against us in the area of our finances. Having control over our finances affects the other influential factors in that it shows we can be trusted, we make good decisions and we are responsible. It also affects the perception others have of us. People tend to treat those with money differently than those that do not. Additionally, our attitude will be positive because having money makes us feel better.

Familiarity — The Enemy of Influence

Can we influence everyone we meet or everyone we have relationship with? It is quite possible, but not likely because there is at least one enemy to the influential person. That enemy is the **spirit of familiarity.** When we become accustomed to being around the same people all of the time we have a tendency to take each other for granted. This explains why family members can be some of the most difficult people in our lives to influence, especially with regards to salvation. When we are taken for granted by our loved ones, friends, co-workers and fellow church members they have actually become seduced by the spirit of familiarity to the point of carelessness and informality. Lack of appreciation towards others will also damage our ability to be influential because their perception of us will have changed over time due to our insensitivity.

Matthew 13: 57-58 — And they were offended in Him. But Jesus said unto them, "A prophet is not without honor, save in his own country, and in his own house." And He did not many mighty works there because of their unbelief. KJV

Jesus himself did very few miracles in his own hometown because of familiarity. This spirit adversely affects credibility, trust and perception. One sure way to combat this spirit in our own lives with respect to our relationships is with gratitude. When we are grateful we will continuously make an effort to show our appreciation for the relationships we have been afforded. Understanding the privilege and blessing in having our various relationships will cause us to maintain an attitude of gratitude and prevent us from taking our loved ones for granted or being neglectful. When we show appreciation towards others our potential to positively influence them becomes more likely.

We should in summary keep in mind these five final points in our efforts towards altering, strengthening and maintaining our influence:

- The greater the number of people that we have **relationship** with along with the amount of **trust** extended will cause increased influence.

- As our **responsibilities** increase, so too our level of influence as well as our sphere of influence.

- Because a rich person or famous person has the opportunity to influence a great many people, their **sphere of influence** becomes enlarged as their popularity increases.

- Influencers should have a greater sense of **responsibility** and guard their **integrity** because of the **perception** held by those they come into contact with, especially those closest to them.

- Because **money** increases the potential for a person to receive additional popularity, **godly character** and wise **decisions** becomes critical ingredients to maintaining one's influence.

Chapter 11

Contrasts — Women In The Bible

When an advertising company wants to repackage a product to boost sales, they oftentimes add "New and Improved" to their labels. I believe that's what God did with the influential trait when He created the woman. Throughout the Bible there are many noteworthy examples of women of influence. Some used negative influences over men and others used their positive influence with men— namely their husbands. Still others used their influence with or over their children. But then there were those women that had influence with God. These women not only used their influence to change their personal lives but they also changed and determined history. Consider the following women influential enough to find their names and their lives recorded in the scriptures.

Eve the first woman, wife and mother; Sarah—Abraham's wife; Moses' sister Miriam; Rebekah the wife of Isaac; Leah and Rachel the wives of Jacob; Ruth and her mother-in-law Naomi; Esther the queen; Jezebel, another queen; Hagar the handmaiden of Sarah; Hannah the mother of Samuel the prophet; Deborah the Judge; Rahab the harlot and mother of Boaz; Michal—David's first wife; Mary the mother of Jesus; Martha and Mary Magdalene servants and followers of Jesus; Elizabeth the mother of John the Baptist; Priscilla a missionary, who traveled and evangelized with her husband Aquila and served Paul the Apostle; and Delilah are those we remember most. Of course one of the most popular romances of the Bible involved a woman named Bathsheba.

There are also the influential nameless women worth listing; Potiphar's wife; the Shulamite woman in the Song of Solomon; King Lemuel's mother who gave him the description of a virtuous woman in Proverbs 31; the Shunammite woman that perceived Elisha's prophetic anointing; the Samaritan woman at Jacob's well; the woman with the issue of blood; the Syrophoenician woman who's daughter was vexed with a devil; the widow with two mites; the woman that was loosed; the woman with the alabaster box and the list goes on. Furthermore, Solomon is careful to warn us about the strange woman, the brawling woman and the results of adultery in the book of Proverbs.

Although this power began with Eve, women throughout history have learned to make use of this God-given trait. All of these notable women had one thing in common; they all used their influence to effect change. No matter what their plight, position, cause or situation they all possessed the ability to invoke changes by using their influence. Each time one of these women used her influence in a positive way, not only was she helped and delivered but her whole family was as well. In some instances an entire nation was spared certain annihilation. On the other hand, those that used their influence for selfish, personal gains and had immoral motives produced unwarranted and disparaging results. Regardless of the outcome, all of these women had some visible form of influence during their lives. Though the results in each case of these women's stories vary by circumstance, they all accomplished their desired objectives whether good or bad.

The next few accounts are of women that used the negative forms of influence. Through each of these stories we will find manipulation, seduction, coercion and enticement in full recognizable operation.

It Runs In The Family

Genesis 16:1-3 — Now Sarah Abram's wife bare him no children: and she had a handmaid, an Egyptian, whose name was Hagar. And Sarah said unto Abram, "Behold now, the Lord hath restrained me from bearing: I pray thee, go in unto my handmaid; it may be that I may obtain children by her." And Abram hearkened to the voice of Sarah. KJV

Sarah had grown weary of waiting on God to give her the son she had been promised and decided to take matters into her own hands. Abraham too, wanted desperately to fulfill the prophecy for his life, that he would be the father of many nations. Sarah played on Abraham's emotions and the fact he desired a son. She offered him a solution he seemingly could not refuse. Sarah, out of her desperation, presents her handmaiden to Abraham and influenced him to impregnate her.

What Sarah was actually operating in was manipulative influence. Notice Sarah first proposes her idea to Abraham and then brings her handmaiden to him. Her seemingly sensible suggestion and subsequent actions produced an outcome, which proved to be detrimental for all involved. Additionally, Sarah's one desperate decision to have a child caused hurt and pain for those closest to her. Hagar eventually loses her job as Sarah's handmaiden. Ishmael, the innocent child in this story is forced to grow up without his father and Abraham had to send his son away all because of Sarah's manipulative ways. One very valuable lesson we can learn from Sarah's story is that we mustn't get ahead of God or try to do God's job for Him.

Sarah eventually becomes pregnant at the age of 90 and the promise of a son is fulfilled. But the manipulative spirit of Sarah didn't stop with Hagar and Ishmael or just because she gave birth to Isaac. That same spirit flowed down to at least the next two generations.

Once Isaac grows to adulthood he marries Rebekah. Rebekah, like her mother-in-law is manipulative too. She gives birth to twin sons, Esau and Jacob. The Bible records that Isaac loved Esau, the firstborn, but Rebekah loved Jacob. Not only does Rebekah become manipulative where her husband is concerned, but she also instructs her son Jacob to deceive his own father.

Genesis 27: 6-8 — And Rebekah spake unto Jacob her son, saying, "Behold, I heard thy father speak unto Esau thy brother, saying 'Bring me venison, and make me savory meat, that I may eat, and bless thee before the Lord before my death.' Now therefore, my son, obey my voice according to that which I command thee." KJV

As the story continues, Jacob manages to fool his father and steals his brother's blessing of course with the help of his mother's convincing enticement. No wonder Jacob continued to have struggles with cheating, stealing and swindling people throughout much of his life. His grandmother, Sarah, had released the manipulative spirit into the family lineage and his mother taught him how to use it.

Jacob's wives, Leah and Rachel, were also manipulative and seducing. Unfortunately, Jacob had been hoodwinked by his father-in-law, married Leah. Jacob's initial intention was to marry Rachel, Leah's younger sister however it was customary in those days for the elder sister to be married first. Leah's father entices Jacob with wine during their wedding feast. Jacob becomes intoxicated and winds up with Leah in his bed instead of Rachel. When Jacob woke up the next morning he realized that he had been tricked. The marriage had been consummated and Jacob was now trapped married to Leah. Leah knew from the beginning of her marriage that Jacob didn't love her but she began bearing children for him, hoping to change his heart. This manipulative tactic did not work then and it will not work now.

Eventually Jacob marries his beloved Rachel, but Rachel has a problem with being able to conceive. Because Rachel wanted desperately to have Jacob's children, she too came up with the same scheme as her predecessor Sarah.

Genesis 30:3-5 — And she said, "Behold my maid Bilhah, go in unto her; and she shall bear upon my knees, that I may also have children by her." And she gave him Bilhah her handmaid to wife: and Jacob went in unto her. And Bilhah conceived, and bare Jacob a son. KJV

Rachel convinces Jacob to have relations with her handmaiden Bilhah in an attempt to compete with her sister. She was very envious of Leah because by this time, Leah had already birthed four of Jacob's sons. Bilhah, Rachel's servant, not only gives birth to one son, but is permitted to be intimate with Jacob again, thus producing a second son. Now the score is 4 sons to 2 in favor of Leah and the situation has really gotten out of control.

Leah, not to be outdone by her sister, decides to use her handmaid in the same manner. Jacob had ceased having intercourse with Leah, but Leah had no problem allowing Zilpah, her handmaiden, to sleep with Jacob. Zilpah, like Bilhah births two more sons for Jacob.

In Leah's final attempt to win the love and affections of Jacob, makes a deal with Rachel. Leah had what Rachel needed and Rachel had what Leah wanted. Rueben, Leah's oldest son, is out in the field one day and returns home with some mandrakes for his mother. Rachel saw Rueben with these precious plants and desired to obtain them from him. During biblical times, it was believed that the root of the mandrake could promote conception. Perhaps this was how Leah was able to bear so many children. Rachel persuades Leah to sell one of Rueben's mandrakes to her. In return, Rachel agrees to permit Leah to spend the night with Jacob one more time.

In total, Leah produced six sons and one daughter for Jacob, but never does achieve her goal of changing Jacob's feelings towards her. And after an awful lot of manipulation, jealousy, competition and desperation by both sisters, Rachel finally becomes pregnant and gives birth to Joseph. Of course Joseph grows up to be hated by his brothers not only for his dreams, but because there was such rivalry and dysfunction in his family before he was born. (I wonder if Joseph referred to Leah as his stepmother or his aunt — just a thought.) Whatever he called her, we can see how seduction, manipulation and enticement played a crucial part in the lives of Sarah, Abraham, Isaac, Rebekah, Jacob, Leah, Rachel, their handmaids and their children.

The Seduction of Sampson

Judges 16: 4 — And it came to pass afterward, that he loved a woman in the valley of Sorek, whose name was Delilah. KJV

Sampson was a Nazarite and a mighty warrior that had been pre-ordained by God to deliver the Israelites from the Philistines. He served as the children of Israel's judge during a twenty-year period although the Philistines ruled over the land. Sampson repeatedly continued to be in conflict with the Philistine people during his reign as the Israelites' leader.

Best known for his superhuman strength, some of Sampson's most notable feats were killing a lion with his bare hands, slaying a thousand men with the jawbone of an ass and carrying the gates of the city of Gaza away on his back.

Sampson however, had a weakness for strange women and in Judges 16 we find the story of a particular woman that deliberately seduced him to utter ruin and an untimely death. A prostitute by profession, Delilah was the infamous femme fatale that seductively influenced Sampson into divulging the secret of his tremendous strength to her. She had been lured through bribery into this evil conspiracy by the lords of the Philistines and by her own greed. Delilah must have found it somewhat challenging and self-gratifying to be given the task of defeating the strongest man in the land as she employed her charm and persistence to ensnare Sampson. Sampson succumbed to Delilah's manipulative scheme eventually losing his strength, his vision and his life.

Proverbs 5:3-5 — For the lips of a strange woman drop as a honeycomb, and her mouth is smoother than oil; but her end is bitter as wormwood, sharp as a two-edged sword. Her feet go down to death; her steps take hold on hell. KJV

The book of Proverbs gives multiple warnings concerning the ways of the strange woman and Delilah was one such woman. Even though Sampson had accomplished incredible feats, killing a lion and single-handedly slaughtering one thousand Philistines, he was no match for Delilah's cunning influence. Delilah understood that she had what it took to bring Sampson down.

This story similarly has the same sequence of events that took place in the Garden of Eden. Eve was first enticed by Adam's enemy to eat of the tree of knowledge of good and of evil. Delilah was enticed by Sampson's enemies. Then there was the introduction of incentives for both women. Delilah's compensation was monetary and Eve's reward was knowledge and to become like God. Next Eve entices her husband while Delilah seduces Sampson. Another noteworthy similarity of these stories is that Satan didn't directly attack Adam's strength or Sampson's, but instead went after their weakness—that weakness being the women in their lives. Keep in mind, strongholds will gain entrance and establish roots at the point of least resistance.

There was however an important difference between these two women. One significant distinction is that Eve was not initially after Adam's strength nor was she intentionally trying to destroy him. Delilah however targeted Sampson's strength, but like Adam it was Sampson's weakness for a woman that in the end caused his demise. Just as Satan manipulated Eve to rob Adam of his dominion in the earth, the lords of the Philistines used Delilah to strip Sampson of his strength and authority.

The enemy will always go after a man's weakness to bring him down and remove him from his position of power. Satan has used women repeatedly throughout history to bring men to utter defeat and destruction and it all started with Eve. In recent history we have numerous accounts of great, influential men that have been involved in scandalous affairs where a woman is either being bribed, supposedly victimized or to blame. Some of these men have been famous athletes, others judges, ambitious politicians, popular pastors and media celebrities.

The man's enemies sometimes promise a woman large sums of money or she is persuaded by a money-hungry lawyer to pursue a civil lawsuit in an attempt to extort the man's wealth and destroy his reputation. She may also play this role for her own selfish greed and notoriety. For most of these women once their assignment is complete they fade off into obscurity and we never hear of them again. Comparably notable is that after Delilah reveals Sampson's secret to the lords of the Philistines we hear of her no further in the scriptures.

Then There Was Jezebel

I Kings 21:25 — But there was none like unto Ahab, which did sell himself to work wickedness in the sight of the Lord, whom Jezebel his wife stirred up. KJV

In this biblical account we find the epitome of the coercive nature employed by Jezebel the queen. "Stirred up" in this passage of scripture is interpreted to mean, "to entice". After the prophet Elijah makes a spectacle out of Jezebel's prophets by completely destroying them she becomes very angry with him. She issues a contract on Elijah's life and as a result the mighty prophet of God ran away and hid out in a cave for forty days. Because Jezebel knew that men were visual, she sent a messenger to Elijah to show him her written command to have him killed. Initially the real purpose of her threat was to instill fear in Elijah to the point that he would become incapable of embarrassing her any more. The fear Elijah experienced was intended to render him completely powerless. Elijah became so frightened, and rightfully so, that he went a day's journey into the wilderness to escape Jezebel's threat. Understand that Elijah had just called down fire from heaven to consume the altar, all of its contents and then commanded the children of Israel to kill 450 of Jezebel's prophets. Prior to that miracle he prophesied to King Ahab, Jezebel's husband, they would be without rain for three years—and the rain ceased! Yet based on this coercive woman's decree Elijah seemingly lost all sense of faith in God and himself.

Jezebel used her position as queen to threaten, scare and kill anyone that got in her way. Her coerciveness was so

The Power of Eve

dangerously effective that even after Elijah withstood 450 prophets of Baal he found himself fleeing away from one evil woman. What's even more startling is in addition to Elijah hiding, there were another one hundred prophets of God huddled up in caves too!

Although God sent the prophet Elijah to Ahab many times during his 22-year reign as king with a message to repent and turn back to God, Ahab was negatively influenced by his wife and continued arrogantly sinning against God. Jezebel's wicked use of her influential power eventually led her and her husband down the path of death and destruction. As a direct result of their combined disobedience, Ahab died miserably in battle and Jezebel fell to her death from the palace balcony and is subsequently eaten by wild dogs.

The Enticement of Herod

Mark 6:22-24 — And the daughter of the said Herodias came in, and danced, and pleased Herod and them that sat with him, the king said unto the damsel, "Ask of me whatsoever thou wilt, and I will give it thee." And he swore unto her, "Whatsoever thou shalt ask of me, I will give it thee, unto the half of my kingdom." And she went forth, and said unto her mother, "What shall I ask?" And she said, "The head of John the Baptist". KJV

That must have been some dance! Herodias had been accustomed to wielding her influence to get what she wanted. When John the Baptist attempted to correct Herodias and her husband concerning their adulterous relationship and subsequent marriage, she became quite agitated. Herodias knew her husband too was extremely angry with John the Baptist and they both wanted him silenced—permanently.

Not only did Herodias use her influence over her husband, she persuasively enlists her daughter Salome to assist her in carrying out this murderous plot. Herodias cleverly contrived a plan and conspires with her daughter to fulfill her husband's wishes. She instructs her daughter to ask for the head of John the Baptist after Herod told her he would give her whatever she wanted up to and including half of his kingdom. John the Baptist was then beheaded upon the indirect request and influence of King Herod's wife, Herodias and the seductive dancing of her daughter Salome.

Elements of Positive Influence

Fortunately we don't have to be persons of prominence, fame or wealth to influence others that are of a greater or higher status—whether from the world's standards or the church's standards. Whether you are found like Ruth, selected like Esther or chosen like Mary, the ability to influence others is within each one of us. Influence is not limited to or controlled by nationality, gender, age or social status. In addition to the factors of influence, there are necessary elements requisite to an individual obtaining a greater level of influence. Position, preparation and purpose all play a role in the influence equation.

God will oftentimes position a person for greatness prior to the actual fulfillment of their purpose. During the preparation phase their influence will gradually increase for the purpose of operating fully in their position. These next three women are examples of how God used position, preparation and purpose to achieve His desire for their lives. And while God used them, they used their influence to produce positive results.

What Ruth, Esther and Mary had in common is that they all started out in obscurity according to man's standards but they were deemed important and significant in the eyes of God. They all were chosen by God to bring salvation to their people and ultimately the world. Esther was selected by King Ahazerus to become his wife and queen of Persia. She ultimately becomes influential in saving her people, the children of Israel. Ruth helped not only herself, but provided for her mother-in-law as well. Because of her loyalty to Naomi and her influence with Boaz, she though not of Jewish descent, is now a matriarch in the lineage of Christ. Later in biblical history, Mary, a virgin girl, is chosen to birth our Lord and Savior Jesus Christ into the world to save all of mankind. All three were elevated from their seemingly normal existence only to be interrupted by God's desire to fulfill His purpose for their lives. Notice too, that all of these women had ties to royalty.

Likewise in modern times, Princess Diana was born a "nobody", but died not only a princess, but as one of the greatest influential women of our time. Both of her sons are now in line to become King of England. Could she have imagined as she was growing up she would one day give birth to kings? Like Mary who birthed Jesus into the world, not only can women have influence in the earth, but we also are carrying the seeds of great future influential people in our wombs.

The Positioning of Ruth

Ruth 2:2 — And Ruth the Moabitess said unto Naomi, "Let me now go to the field, and glean ears of corn after him in whose sight I shall find grace." And she said unto her, "Go my daughter." KJV

Prior to Ruth's positioning, tragedy struck not only her life but also her sister-in-law Orpah's and her mother-in-law Naomi's. They had all tragically lost their husbands. The Bible is not clear as to what exactly happened to their husbands but we do know that they died. Naomi decides to return to her homeland of Judah and Ruth opts to go with her. Once they arrive in Judah, Naomi seeks out a relative of her late husband's by the name of Boaz.

Even though tragedy had come to Ruth's life, she perseveres and finds herself positioned at the right place at the right time. Ruth operated with humility along with a positive confession despite a terrible turn of events that had transpired in her life. Ruth is discovered while in a strange land, serving a strange God in a stranger's field. She was minding her own business, caring for her mother-in-law and just trying to survive when Boaz found her.

Boaz was wealthy and owned a great deal of land. Ruth is instructed by her mother-in-law to glean in Boaz's fields in order to obtain food. Soon, Boaz noticed Ruth working in his field and inquired of her from his servants. Because Ruth assumed the responsibility of taking care of Naomi, she gained favor with Boaz. Boaz then commands his field hands to leave more corn for her to harvest than before. Bear in mind that responsibility is one of the factors of influence.

Because of the influential power Naomi had with Ruth as a direct result of their relationship, she was able to coach Ruth into her destiny in spite of their losses. Boaz then makes the decision to marry Ruth according to Jewish custom although she was not of Jewish heritage. What is most notable about Ruth was she was not a person of any particular significance at the beginning of her story, but by the end, she had not only married Boaz who was rich, but becomes linked to the lineage of Jesus. Ruth's decision to remain loyal to her mother-in-law positioned her to become the wife of Boaz, the mother of Obed and chosen by God to be the great-grandmother of King David.

The Preparation of Esther

Esther 2:17 — And the king loved Esther above all the women, and she obtained grace and favor in his sight more than all the virgins; so that he set the royal crown upon her head, and made her queen instead of Vashti. KJV

Esther's story is not only one of influence, but she also teaches us about the necessity of preparation, unwavering courage and the importance of positioning. With the help and encouragement from her Uncle Mordecai, Esther is presented with the opportunity to become the next queen over provinces extending from India to Ethiopia.

Vashti, who was the first queen and wife of King Ahasuerus, was dethroned when she used her influence in a negative way. Vashti had defied her husband's wishes to join him at a feast he was hosting. Her refusal caused great embarrassment for the king. King Ahasuerus' counsel members became fearful and reasoned that Vashti's defiance would influence all of the other wives to rebel against their husbands too. Evidently Vashti didn't realize just how powerful her position of influence was. Nevertheless, Vashti's error was to Esther's benefit.

King Ahasuerus sends out a decree to find a new queen to replace Vashti. Mordecai realized that his niece had something special and convinced Esther to get in the running. (This was the first beauty pageant of sorts.) Esther's preparation to become the next queen required education for an entire year of the social etiquettes of her day prior to being presented to the king as his potential bride. Once the opportunity presented itself, Esther's beauty won King Ahasuerus over. More important than the influence of her beauty, was the influence of the favor of God on her life. She shows us that preparation prior to our assignment is necessary to fulfilling God's purpose for our lives. Furthermore, during the preparation process her positioning was also being established.

The need for her influence came in to play at two specific times; first when she was presented to the king and secondly, once she became queen, she desired to save her people from Haman's plot to wipe out the children of Israel. She risks her own life in order to save her people but it was her influence that got the job done. Notice too, that Esther does not use her femininity or her influence in a lurid way. Her motives were not of a selfish nature. She only used her position of influence for the betterment of her people.

The Purpose of Mary

Mary, the mother of Jesus, was chosen by God to bring the Savior into the world. Like Moses' mother, Mary too had to hide her son from the authorities until he was of a certain age. Mary's purpose was not only to give birth to Jesus, but in addition to rearing him properly according to Jewish traditions, she also ushered him into his ministry. Using her motherly influence, she prompts her son into performing his first miracle.

John 2:3-5 — And when they wanted wine, the mother of Jesus saith unto him, "They have no wine." Jesus saith unto her, "Woman, what have I to do with thee? Mine hour is not yet come." His mother saith unto the servants, "Whatsoever he saith unto you, do it." KJV

In this passage of scripture, Jesus and his mother were attending a wedding feast. The overseer of the celebration had miscalculated the number of guests in attendance. Because of this error, they ran out of wine prematurely, not having a solution. Mary turns to Jesus and explains to him there is no more wine. Jesus, seemingly irritated with his mother for concerning him with this issue, says it's none of his concern. Although Jesus spoke to his mother in an apparently impolite manner, Mary gives the impression of ignoring Jesus' sharp response. She knew that it was time for her son to be revealed as the Messiah. Mary abruptly turns to the servants and instructs them to do whatever Jesus says do, completely disregarding her son's discontented remark. She influences not only the servants, but Jesus as well. Jesus tells the servants to gather six water pots, fill them with water and deliver them to the governor of the feast. Miraculously, Jesus had turned the water into wine and this is the first recorded miracle performed by Jesus. Mary, because she was not only his mother, but also a woman of influence, understood her son's purpose in the earth and guides Jesus into his ministry.

She Influenced God

Influence comes from God as stated in the previous chapters, but it is important for us to know that we can actually influence God to move on our behalf. Keep in mind that influence is the ability to affect a change with little or no effort or to have an effect on the condition or development of.

God wants us to be co-laborers with Him regarding the purpose for our lives. Because this is true, we can become partners with God and recipients of the blessings of God. He is not our puppet though. God is our Father and cannot be manipulated. As any good father wants the best for his children, God does what he does for us because He's motivated by love and purpose. We must therefore examine our motives for wanting Him to change or help us in our situations. Our motives must be pure and unselfish in order for God to assist us.

Hannah's Cry

I Samuel 1:10 & 17 — And she was in bitterness of soul, and prayed unto the Lord, and wept sore. 17 - Then Eli answered and said, "Go in peace: and the God of Israel grant thee thy petition that thou hast asked of him." KJV

Hannah's story is another biblical account of two wives married to the same husband. Although Elkanah had two wives, he favored Hannah more than his other wife Peninnah. As in the story of Leah and Rachel, Hannah was the woman most loved by her husband, but was also the one unable to bear children. Peninnah, on the other hand, like Leah was able to have many children and taunted Hannah because of her barrenness. Hannah however, continued to be faithful in prayer and worship to the Lord, observing the feasts and sacrificial ceremonies. Each year during their annual time of worship at the tabernacle, Hannah cried and prayed so fervently to the Lord for a son until one day God answered her prayer. She vows to give her son back to God to be raised as a prophet. One thing is certain, Hannah knew she had greatness locked up inside of her and she also understood the influential significance of her vow.

God considers a vow legally binding and a very serious offering of commitment and consecration. Her petition pulled at God's heartstrings because He knew the sincerity of her request. Though Hannah's desire for a son may have at first seemed like a selfish request, on the contrary, once she promised to dedicate her son to the work of the Lord, her plea became quite selfless. This is positive influence in totality. What's more, Hannah's prayer was reciprocal in nature. Although she was asking something from God for herself, she vows to return the gift back to God for His use.

God has a special adoration for sons, especially when they are offered as a sacrifice to fulfill His purpose. Hannah knew this and used sound reasoning, her understanding of God's heart and prayer in order to influence God to grant her the son she so desperately prayed for. After she gives birth to Samuel, she keeps her vow and returns him to the care of Eli the priest. Because she kept her promise to God, God then blesses her with three more sons and two daughters.

All of these women had it. Although some used their influential ability to create negative scenarios, those whom released their influence for the greater good yielded positive results not only for themselves, but for those they cared about. We see through these examples influence used in practical yet powerful ways. We may not be called to rescue an entire nation, such as Esther, or give birth to kings like Ruth and Mary, but we all have an assignment for which practical application of our influence will be a tool of great significance.

Chapter 12

The War — Women and the Church

So where do we go from here? We now see how the events that took place in the garden have gradually led us down the path of death, decay and destruction in our current society. Statistically speaking, our world seems to be headed for ultimate ruin. We also see the results of having received incorrect information, starting with Eve. Conversely, we also find the answer to our current dilemmas in that same garden, which can significantly assist us in restoring our families, communities and nation back to the place of its original intent.

What is at stake is our ability to positively influence our situations towards the abundant life we were promised through the scriptures. Choosing to no longer be conformed to the "world system", and our gained awareness of the seductive satanic forces, we can rise above living beneath our inherited privileges. Though psychological programming and conditioned response have played a major role in convincing us of what is acceptable, introspection and reflection becomes necessary in determining the changes we perhaps need to make. Have we been passive, perfectionists, or martyrs, manipulative or controlling? What erroneous thinking have we accepted and adopted as truth? Expecting better or different results can be realized once we make the decision to change. Furthermore, the behaviors we may have previously employed should no longer have dominion in our lives.

The truth about Eve's mistake and the mistakes made by other women throughout the Bible, have assisted us in seeing how important our choices really are. Eve had an ability to influence not only her husband but also her entire family. Like Eve, women are either the strongest link or the weakest link within the family because of our influential trait. Depending on a woman's self-assessment, she can be quite influential or very easily controlled. Her ability to positively influence those within her care will ultimately affect the wholeness of the family structure. Therefore, the woman's role with regards to this powerful attribute is important to grasp for the ensuing battle.

Genesis 3:14 — And I will put enmity between thee and the woman, and between thy seed and her seed; it shall bruise thy head, and thou shalt bruise his heel. KJV

Once Adam and Eve sinned, God's judgment proceeded. Because Satan attacked the woman, God determines that she will now become his perpetual enemy and he hers. God, however, has equipped women to be victorious with a most powerful weapon. Furthermore, the enemy not only continues to make war with women, our children are now his targets too. His goal of course is to ultimately destroy God's creation—the family, therefore, it becomes extremely imperative for marriages and families to remain united on one accord.

In today's society, the family has taken on different structural combinations. Families can be made up of single parent families, families with stepparents, adoptive parents, foster parents and yours-mine-and-ours parents.

Whatever the structure of your family, it's vitally important that it stays intact. Our belief systems, life skills, and relational training are all defined within the family unit. A sense of belonging and an understanding of identity are also developed. The ability to successfully relate to other people, especially in group-settings, such as, school or the work environment are taught and established through family interaction. Our core values, morals, discipline, self-respect and respect for others have their foundation in our rearing and are all vitally essential elements to a thriving society. How the husband treats his wife weighs heavily on the outcome of her sons' and daughters' perception of themselves. It will also dictate how they treat others, especially once they've established their own family units.

We must recognize though, the family has been under attack since the "fall of man". If the family is destroyed, society as we know it, will assuredly self-destruct. And if the family is on Satan's hit list, it must be much more important than two parents and some children.

Another look at the sequence of events that transpired after sin entered the world, find Adam and Eve's roles and responsibilities changed and diminished to a lower order. Adam, by the sweat of his brow, tilled the ground, which God had cursed. Eve would bear children experiencing the pains of labor and delivery. Once Cain and Abel were born, their rivalry was a direct result of the lower nature now having dominion over humanity. Not only did Satan beguile Eve, he moved on to her children and was successful in deceiving Cain to kill his brother Abel. Since that time, murder becomes Satan's device to kill the seed of the woman. The war is now launched against the family and has been raging ever since.

Unfortunately, in present-day society, abortion is the killing of the seed and of our future generations. Abortion has taken hold and is engulfing our nation. Sadly, Satan is not to blame with respect to us killing our children. Again, all he's done is fed us a lie. We've bought into the falsehood that we as women have a right to choose what happens to our bodies. In this respect, we have become like God, determining who lives and who dies. We've opted to murder our unborn children ignorantly destroying a part of our selves because it has become acceptable. Remember, we have to be careful of what becomes acceptable.

Not only is abortion destroying our future families, it's only one of the many atrocities in our modern day society. With the constant rise in the number of women going to prison, many innocent children are growing up without their mothers. Furthermore, while domestic violence is ultimately teaching our children how to disrespect and injure women, pornography is ripping at the very fabric of our marriages and culture. Undoubtedly, the war against the woman and her seed is fierce, but we still have a weapon and we still have a choice.

Unity is Key

One defense against the destruction of the family is unity. Harmony in our families should be our goal. Where harmony is there is balance. Our marriages and families were originally intended to operate in harmonious stability.

Psalm 133:1-3 — Behold, how good and how pleasant it is for brethren to dwell together in unity! KJV

Harmony and cooperation is God's ultimate goal for our families because it produces unity. Satan is acutely aware of the tremendous influential power of a unified family. The cohesive blending of a family unit is what makes a household function properly. As each member fulfills their designated role, the family then becomes a productive unit. The children are nurtured and grow to be healthy, whole individuals.

Once the children reach adult age, they move on to create their own family units. The cycle continues and the earth becomes populated with more... and more... and more of God's ultimate creation.

While God commands the blessing at the place of unity, the enemy fights us at this same place. Satan does not want us to be blessed or to have healthy relationships. When our relationships are healthy, the effectiveness of our witness as Christians will increase thereby positively influencing those we come into contact with.

Your Testimony

Revelation 12:11 — And they overcame him by the blood of the Lamb, and by the word of their testimony. KJV

In addition to the attack on the family, on an individual level, whether saved or unsaved, we all have our own personal battles to contend with. Though this is true, Jesus shows us the way to victorious living. He was and still is unquestionably the most influential person in history. Through Jesus' teachings, miracles, crucifixion and resurrection, we have an example of what real influence is.

As believers, we too, should be extremely influential people. However, the amount of influence you have is predicated on your willingness to change, while allowing God to have priority and preeminence in your life. Because of the greatness inside of us, Satan has been after our influence all along. His aim is to disarm or at least pervert this powerful weapon we all possess. Our testimony then becomes our most powerful witnessing tool. It has the ability to steer others in the direction of Christ. Tied directly to the effectiveness of our testimony is our influence. Your testimony becomes your marketing strategy and advertising campaign, while your influence is the force working behind the scenes.

People are motivated to "buy into" a product they know works. Because "word of mouth" is the most successful marketing strategy there is, our testimony must be utilized to lead others to Christ. Not only is sharing our testimony necessary, but more importantly, living what we profess is the vital link and proof to win the unsaved.

Many people in the world today are suffering with depression, low self-esteem, addictions, health problems and a variety of other issues. And we hold the answer to their deliverance. Become more willing to share with others the goodness and faithfulness of God. Let them know what God has done for you in your life. Quite simply, people are changed and hope is stirred just by knowing someone else has been delivered, healed or restored.

II Corinthians 5:18 & 20a — And all things are of God, who hath reconciled us to himself by Jesus Christ, and hath given to us the ministry of reconciliation. 20a. Now then we are ambassadors for Christ. KJV

Every believer has been called to be a minister of reconciliation, bringing the unsaved back into right relationship with God. Further deciphering of this scripture defines an ambassador as a high-ranking official sent to be a diplomatic representative of a nation or a kingdom. Diplomacy is the skill of handling relationships without arousing hostility, while reconciliation is the ability to restore harmony, friendship or communion. What an awesome responsibility God has given us! Moreover, he has empowered us and entrusted us through the vehicle of influence to get the job done.

We must therefore guard our testimonies, realizing our personal victories over adversities are what gives others hope. Through the influence of our testimonies, people will be persuaded to give their lives to Christ. Protecting our testimonies becomes extremely imperative because it's what gives us credibility and causes our influence to work.

To enhance the effectiveness of our testimony we must again address the topic of appearance and attitude. Oftentimes it's our outward appearance and countenance people see first before a word is spoken. You never get a second chance to make a first impression. The Bible instructs Christian women to dress modestly. Though we don't want to become overly preoccupied with our outward appearance, but instead focus more on our inward beauty radiating through.

If we exemplify the joy of the Lord, others will want what we have. The silent signals previously discussed demonstrate to those in our sphere of influence how we really feel about our relationship with God. This is vital to influencing others to become saved. Because people respond based on their emotions, a positive attitude goes a long way. Pleasant people attract others and the unsaved are looking for encouragement and hope. They are also watching how you handle life's challenges. Keep in mind that influence is free flowing and yours is working even when you're not consciously aware of it.

God's Woman of Influence

Revelation 12:17 — And the dragon was wroth with the woman, and went to make war with the remnant of her seed, which keep the commandments of God, and have the testimony of Jesus Christ. KJV

Satan's two-fold plan is quite simplistic. Destroy the family and keep the church divided. He's only successful with our cooperation. Figuratively, the woman in Revelation 12 is the church and the remnant refers to those that are saved. Ironically, the church is referred to in the feminine gender throughout the Bible. This being the case, not only is it Satan's intention to make war with women on an individual level, but his plan is also to destroy the church—God's woman of influence. The church is only as strong as its families. Destroy families and the church will also eventually be destroyed.

If Eve had the power of influence over Adam to cause him to sin, surely she has the power through influence to bring him back to God again. And the church, God's woman of influence, has the capability and power of influencing mankind back to God. This is the revelation in the garden. The Garden of Eden was where it all started, but the Garden of Gethsemane is where it all ended.

Though we lost our right standing in the first garden through the tree of knowledge of good and evil, we have been restored through Jesus Christ, which gives us the right to the tree of life, the second forbidden tree. Although we were forbidden from partaking of the tree of life after the original sin, we can now regain our rightful relationship with God and obtain eternal life through Jesus.

Revelation 12:13 — And when the dragon saw that he was cast to earth, he persecuted the woman (the Church) which brought forth the man-child. KJV

Since its inception, the Christian church has suffered continual persecution. From the persecution by Saul of Tarsus, the Crusades, the Holocaust, and church burnings during the Civil Rights era of the 1960's, to the tearing down of Christian artifacts from our government buildings in recent years, the church has had her share of attacks. She is, however, God's woman of immense influence and will continue to be until Jesus returns for her.

Although the church collectively is God's woman of influence, we must realize individually that we are the "church". This is why influence is such an important weapon to learn to develop. We are Christ's representatives. As representatives it is our character, conduct and example that will either lead someone to Christ or keep them from receiving salvation.

Luke 17:20-21 – And when he was demanded of the Pharisees, when the kingdom of God should come, he answered them and said, "The kingdom of God cometh not with observation; neither shall they say, 'Lo here!' or 'Lo there!' for, behold, the kingdom of God is within you". KJV

Certainly, we are the church and the kingdom of God is within every believer. Although we may sometimes think it's the church's responsibility to fix what is wrong with our families and our communities, it is very much within our grasp to change our current situations and conditions. We are able and quite capable of changing our society for the better. We just have to use our influence.

Conclusion

Though my initial assignment of leading my husband back to the Lord is complete, I have not ceased being his helpmeet and the most influential woman in his life. That assignment will only be complete through the separation of death.

Our lives are much different now in comparison to the early stages of our relationship. What a journey it has been! And though we have had our share of tests and challenges, God has remained faithful through it all.

I pray that through my testimony and the lessons about Eve's life, that you too will become a person of great influence. We can change our individual worlds as well as the world at large through this most tremendous ability. Continue to reread sections of this book to assist you in becoming the influential person God has created you to be.

Sources

Domestic Violence —
American Medical Association, National Clearinghouse for the Defense of Battered Women Statistics Packet: 3rd Edition, September 1995.
National Organization for Women, "Violence Against Women: A National Crime Victimization Survey Report", U.S. Department of Justice, Washington, D.C., January 1994.

Sexual Exploitation of Women —
Dushman, Candi. "'Stop Pretending.'" World Magazine. August 5, 2000.
"Sexuality, Contraception, and the Media." American Academy of Pediatrics Committee on Public Education. January 2, 2001.
Galllagher, Steve. "The Greatest Threat to the Church Today". American Family Association, August 18, 2003.

Women in Prison —
Bureau of Justice Statistics, Compendium of Federal Justice Statistics, 2003 (Washington, DC: US Dept. of Justice, Oct. 2005), p. 108, Table 7.10; Harrison, Paige M. & Allen J. Beck, PhD, Bureau of Justice Statistics, Prisoners

in 2004 (Washington DC: US Department of Justice, Oct. 2005), p. 9, Table 13.

Amnesty International, "Not Part of My Sentence: Violations of the Human Rights of Women in Custody" (Washington, DC: Amnesty International, March 1999), p.26.

John Irwin, Ph.D., Vincent Schiraldi, and Jason Ziedenberg, America's One Million Nonviolent Prisoners (Washington, DC: Justice Policy Institute, March 1999), pgs. 6-7.

Single Family Home —
"Historical Income Tables-Families," Bureau of the Census, www.census.gov, Last revised October 4, 1999.

Census Brief CENBR/97-1, Bureau of the Census, www.census.gov, September 1997.

McKenna, Theresa, "The Hidden Mission Field," Winepress Publishing, 1999.

Kliff, Barry, "Heading Toward a Fatherless Society", MSNBC News, www.msnbc.com, March 31, 1999.

"American Agenda," World News Tonight with Peter Jennings, December 13, 1994.

Abortions and Teen Pregnancy —
"A Few Facts About Illegitimacy," Family Research Council, www.frc.org, January 1997.

Press-Release (CB99-213), U.S. Census Bureau's Public Information Office, December 20, 1999.

Sources:

Abortions and Teen Pregnancy —
Alan Guttmacher Institute, "Facts in Brief: Induced Abortion," 2002.

Center for Disease Control and Prevention, "Abortion Surveillance Report," November 25, 2005.

Eating Disorders & Weight Obsession –
Center for Disease Control and Prevention, National Center for Health Statistics, "Body Weight Status of Adults: United States, 1998-98," Charlotte Schoenborn, Patricia Adams, and Patricia Barnes, NCHS Web site.

About the Author

Deanna Manley has served as the Minister of Outreach at her local church since 2002. She has also facilitated Serenity meetings, Christ-centered 12-Step recovery groups in her community. Additionally, she has participated in civic activities, including public hearings, marches and voter registration drives. For the past 8 years she has ministered at recovery houses, shelters, prisons and churches to hundreds of men and women with a message of deliverance through her own personal testimony.

To schedule speaking engagements you may go to www.powerofeve.com.

Printed in the United States
64356LVS00002BD/184-375